PERSPECTIVES

ON ORAL

INTERPRETATION

Essays and Readings

Edited by

JOHN W. GRAY
Auburn University
Auburn, Alabama

Burgess Publishing Company

426 South Sixth Street • Minneapolis, Minn. 55415

Preface

There is no worse arrangement than for one to make pre-
tensions to the spirit of a thing while the sense and letter
of it are not clear to him.

Goethe

One definite indication of the healthy state of affairs in the field of oral interpretation is the multitude of diverse opinions and questions which are stirring the academic waters and creating real interest among teachers and serious students of the art. The variety of essays and readings contained in this book attempts to present a few of these questions and offers some helpful discussion of the possible answers. Each chapter is complete within itself but makes no pretense of being exhaustive.

The contributors have presented a definite set of viewpoints and opinions concerning selected aspects of oral interpretation the under-lying philosophy being that many students practice the art of oral interpretation with very little understanding of the theory and process involved. We felt a need for readings in depth outside the usual discussion of skills. A similar feeling has been evident in the speech communication area with the new emphasis on theory and process in communication.

Inspired by Gertrude Johnson's earlier book entitled *Studies in the Art of Interpretation* (1940), this text is a cooperative effort of experienced teachers of oral interpretation. Each contributor has chosen interest areas and problem areas of the discipline and has given of his knowledge and experience to make this a flexible book which lends itself to a variety of needs. We believe it would serve well as supplementary reading for the beginning oral interpretation course. The chapters could be used in full or in part as outside reading whenever the teacher feels the need for depth and extended discussion of specific areas of theory and process. It also might be used alone or as a companion text for use with anthologies in the advanced undergraduate and graduate courses.

There is a great divergence of practice among teachers of oral interpretation as to the organization and activity in the advanced courses. We believe this is a healthy situation, and we hope the readings in this book will provide a variety of materials for these courses and a valuable spring board to stimulate discussion and investigation by the student. However it is used we feel it will widen the student's perspectives in oral interpretation.

John W. Gray

Acknowledgments

Many persons have assisted in producing this text. The editor wishes to thank his colleagues in the Department of Speech at Auburn University for their suggestions and assistance in the early stages of the manuscript; Linda Mallory for her efforts in typing and proof reading; and to the Burgess editorial staff for valuable criticism and counsel. Finally, the editor wishes to acknowledge the patience and encouragement of his wife, Polly.

JWG

Contents

Chapter I

THE PROCESS: ORAL INTERPRETATION AS COMMUNICATION

John W. Gray

Oral Interpretation is a process which can be taught and learned. This first chapter introduces a few of the basic ingredients of the process in light of current communication theory.

$\mathbf{B}$elieving that a better understanding of the process and nature of an art leads to improved chances for successful performance, it seems appropriate. in a text of this nature, to devote this first chapter to an investigation and discussion of oral interpretation in its most basic terms. This chapter, therefore, will discuss oral interpretation as a process of oral communication, its uniqueness and certain concepts basic to any study of the art.

A study of oral interpretation as a communication process is nothing new. For many years oral interpretation, along with public address and theatre, has been viewed as a discipline concerned primarily with the development of oral skills. This emphasis in itself indicates a "process view". Currently the area of public address has made substantial progress and development by adapting and using the new research findings provided by a relatively new emphasis on the behavioral approach to speech communication[1]. Oral interpretation and theatre have remained rather disinterested in the current research in communication methods and processes. They have always considered themselves an art and, although not opposed to certain types of investigation, have been reluctant to expose their sacred areas (aesthetic distance, empathy, literary experience.) to scientific experimentation. Although I doubt seriously that scientific investigation will provide many breathtaking revelations in all these areas, I would suggest that the negative attitude and the disinterested condition hinder and often prevent excellent possibilities for research in oral interpretation.

An examination of oral interpretation textbooks published before 1960 reveals that much of the material concerned with oral reading skills is identical to the materials found in public speaking texts (audience analysis, bodily action, empathy, voice and diction, stage fright.) The remainder of the material (imagery, literary structure, aesthetics, author's intent.) reflects the influences of early literary texts. These influences are understandable in light of the historical development of oral interpretation. The speech arts grew up together, influencing heavily each other's development. Only in the past few years have the separate speech areas begun their own serious experimentation and research of processes basic to their area. It is encouraging in the modern speech department to see the areas of speech correction, audiology, and speech communication taking the lead in developing new insights through the behavioral approach and experimental research. It is regretable that oral interpretation and theatre have not taken a greater interest in such studies. I must hasten to say that all aspects of oral interpretation may not lend themselves to scientific examination. We may discover, however, that the new developments in the areas of speech communication and psychology have much to offer the student of oral interpretation as he attempts to answer such questions as: (1) How effective is oral interpretation as a mode of literary study? (2) What is empathic response? (3) How valuable is a study of audience behavior and attitude change to the oral interpreter? (4) What communication barriers are involved in the writer-reader-audience relationship? (5) Does an introduction hinder or enhance a reading?*

Much of the evidence we use in support of our current answers to these questions has been gleaned from either isolated personal experiences or paraphrased from the "slick" phrases found in early oral interpretation and speech textbooks. Our hypotheses arising from personal experiences must be tested and our overworked phrases and terms examined and, possibly, re-defined. Not only must we investigate the current writing and research in such allied areas as psychology, literature, aesthetics, philosophy, and linguistics, but we must initiate research and find answers to questions which plague our discipline. In some areas we are making valuable headway but these studies and writings are few in number and are originating generally from the same sources. If we intend to develop as a discipline and to expand and strengthen our graduate work, we must be active in all areas of research and investigation.

THE ORAL INTERPRETATION PROCESS

Oral interpretation is a complex and variable process, and I would argue that the teacher and student of oral interpretation are already process-oriented individuals. Any discussion or explanation of the development of oral skill in reading is based on process. Berlo, in his discussion of the human communication process, states that if we decide to accept a phenomenon as a process, we view its events and relationships as "dynamic, on-going, ever-changing, continuous." He goes on to say that when we label something a process, we also mean that it "does not have *a* beginning, *an* end, a fixed sequence of events. It is not static at rest. It is moving. The elements within a process interact; each affects all the others."[2]   This is surely true of

---

*The remaining chapters of this text will discuss these questions.

oral interpretation. Neither the action nor the response is ever exactly the same. We cannot isolate the beginning and the end, nor can we list all the active elements at work during the process. However, if we decide to talk about the process of oral interpretation, we have no alternative but to make arbitrary choices of the potentially relevant elements involved, and isolate these for the purpose of analyzing and communicating about the process. This ends in a static analysis of a dynamic process, that despite its limitations, provides a system for focusing our attention on selected variables at work in the oral interpretation process. This method often ends in a model of the process. The model in Figure 1 will serve as an illustration.[3]

The boundaries on this model have been set a great distance apart in order to include more of the relevant elements. The point at which the writer encountered the original idea in his experience is the beginning, and the response of the oral interpreter's audience is the end. The left channel represents the variables which may act as either barriers or aids to the communication, affecting each step of the process. The right channel represents the varied mediums for encoding and decoding the message. The author, due to his unique ability to perceive, views life's experiences and assesses their significance. He selects from these experiences those whose truth he wishes to communicate. He then imitates these experiences through his selected medium of expression (poetry, prose, drama). The author's creative work is then read and analyzed by the reader who decodes the message in terms of his own experiences. The reader in turn encodes this message into verbal, vocal, and bodily action which takes the form of oral interpretation. And, of course, each member of the audience decodes the message in terms of his own experiences and responds accordingly. We can see that each decoder is trying to receive the message in the purest form possible; having as his objective a direct line of communication from the author's insight to the audience's response. The greater the insight and ability of the writer, reader, and audience the more complete will be the revelation.

There are three major concepts in this oral interpretation process which require explanation and examination: (1) the encoder is attempting to communicate experience, (2) the encoder's message is a complex of attitudes, (3) the encoder's final goal is a "total response."

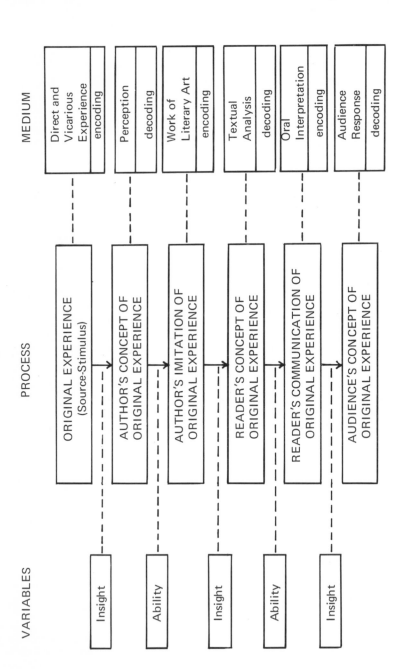

MEDIUM

PROCESS

VARIABLES

FIGURE 1 A General Model of Oral Interpretation as Communication

COMMUNICATION OF EXPERIENCE

Literature has often been defined as an imitation of life; the writer imitating life's experiences and the reader imitating the imitation. Plato thought this mirror-reflector the author holds up to nature incurably defective. He did not think that a writer could symbolize an accurate image of reality. Max Eastman puts it this way: "If the poet can communicate to you, by lulling your body with meter and arousing your mind with metaphor, the refined essential quality of any genuine moment of his inner or outer life, or any imagined life, that is enough. Don't ask for more. If you get something more, it is so much velvet."[4] There are also those who say experience can never be communicated. Their major contention is that the meaning we discover in an experience is always the meaning we put there. Although the statement is essentially true, we must not be led to believe that only objective and external meanings are available for communication. It is true that once we verbalize an event, it is no longer the same event but an imitation of the event. Any verbalization, however, whether written or spoken, must be recognized for its value and contribution to understanding regardless of its purity. For that matter, any attempt at communication must be judged in terms of response. When a musician plays his music or an oral interpreter reads from creative literature, the likeness he makes to experience is not purely sensory, nor is it purely intellectual; it is a synthesis, and what we recognize as "meaning" always carries both the denotative and connotative elements. Both elements are learned through experience and can be used to create an imitation of experience. In literature no one really expects the flawless image of nature, but most readers appreciate the glimpses of reality afforded by a good writer. The same, I imagine, is true of oral interpreters. The audience often forgives the reader for small technical mistakes and less than graceful performances provided the interpretations offer valuable experiences and insights into the literature.

THE MESSAGE

The second concept involves the content of the message communicated by the oral interpreter. Most available definitions of oral interpretation tell us that we communicate the intellectual, emotional, and aesthetic content of literature.[5] Although we may not consider this the final word on the message communicated by the oral interpreter, I do think these terms are serviceable and convenient for a discussion of the process.

Intellectual

When we speak of the intellectual, we mean that the author uses his work to present ideas of intellectual and social significance. Due to the fact that the writer must be selective in choosing general ideas and theories that influence society, we might call his intellectual message a personal criticism of life. It is, therefore, the task of the oral interpreter to seek the author's original intent and to present his criticism as vividly and honestly as possible.

Emotional

When we speak of communicating the emotional content of literature, we mean the psychological appeals used by the author to heighten the effect and vivify the experience for the reader. In any creative art, understanding goes beyond mere comprehension of information. Bare experience cannot be communicated free of attitudes. So the writer of creative literature not only seeks the communication element or logical content which might prove common to both him and his readers, but is just as concerned with the degree to which he is able to select and heighten the effect of this element. Tolstoy explains the emotional content in this manner:

> To evoke in oneself a feeling one has once experienced, and having waked it in oneself, then by means of movements, line, colors, sounds, or forms expressed in words, so to transmit that feeling that others may experience the same feeling—this is the activity of art.
>
> Art is a human activity, consisting in this, that one man consciously, by means of certain external signs, hands on to others feelings he has lived through, and that people are infected by these feelings, and also experience them.[6]

In this passage Tolstoy emphasizes his belief that the activity of art is based primarily on "feeling." We might also say that the oral interpreter's primary concern is with "feeling." Heightening the effect of the intellectual or literal meaning is one of our unique concerns. The content or idea is provided by the author and is gained by the oral interpreter through detailed analysis and close association with the literature. The degree to which the oral interpreter is able to heighten the effect of this message, within the limits of what he has decided is the author's original intent, is directly related to his success in interpreting orally. Although his content is prescribed by the author, this does not mean that the oral interpreter is not an active, creative participant in the literary experience. It simply means that, like the performer of music, his talent and ability are brought to bear on the literary piece in such a way as to enhance and intensify the composer's art. The result is a combining of the composer's art with the performer's art in, hopefully, a full and satisfying revelation of human experience.

When we speak of seeking the author's intent we are not saying the oral interpreter must submit in limited obedience to the declaration of the author. We mean that the author's words and medium must be seen as an arena for the real drama which is the revelation of the experience. The oral interpreter's obligation is to recognize the author's words for what they are—stimuli, to point to their presence, and then to join their action. Then, upon joining the action, he must be a willing and responsive participant in the surprises and possibilities presented by the experience. In this manner the static apprehension of reality, presented by symbols on the page (with their obvious values), is transformed into a dynamic and vital apprehension of life—the living and changing human experience. The "truth" of the literature is revealed, not in terms of static data, but in dramatic action.

Aesthetic

The third aspect communicated is the aesthetic content. As the emotional content concerns itself primarily with the heightening of the experience, the aesthetic concerns itself with the element of selectivity. John T. Marshman states that the oral interpreter must "vitalize anew the author's thought, mood and intent; reconstruct appreciatively what the author as a permanent artist creates in the pages of literature."[7] The literary artist selected carefully the artistic elements to be included and excluded, as well as the artistic method of combining and unifying these elements to produce aesthetic emotion. The oral interpreter must first discover ways of expressing them to an audience. This aesthetic emotion is so closely woven into the fabric of the intellectual and emotional content that it is all but impossible to separate them. The only general distinction we might make here between the emotional content and the aesthetic emotion is in terms of the latter being primarily an appreciatory experience. Our emotional response to a literary work is not motivated solely by our interest in the plot and our identification and involvement with the characters, but also by the pleasure we receive upon contemplating the writer's art. Bacon and Breen expressed it well when they noted that the "particular pleasure that human beings take in the apprehension of well-ordered, meaningful relations, this generalized thrill that comes with the appreciation of the organized unity of a play or a poem or a novel has been called an aesthetic emotion."[8]

The appreciation of a work of art is heightened by an analysis of the artistic form and purpose employed by the writer. This would include a careful study of how the author achieved individuality through the proper use of such elements as style, structure, sound, imagery, rhythm, symbols, and figures of speech.

This study of the particulars is only valuable when it ends in an awareness of the relationships unifying them. This *gestalt* must be actively sought by the oral interpreter and he must attempt to organize his impressions into a complete and satisfying experience.

TOTAL RESPONSE

To be truly successful as an oral interpreter we must seek a "total response" to the author's message, and, in a strict sense, the "message" of the author is the total of his literary piece. What he has to say he has said in the work itself. Any explication on his part is repetitious. He is the source-encoder and has chosen and used his method of artistic expression. Berlo tells us that three factors need to be considered in discussing a message: (1) message code, (2) message content, and (3) message treatment.[9] The message code for the literary artist is language (more specifically the written language with its letters, words, sentences and their arrangement). All writers use the same essential code; their art lies in the effective use of structural syntax and their ability to perceive and communicate human experience. The total message content includes the intellectual, emotional, and aesthetic material which the author desires to present, including any inferences he wishes to make or criticisms he wishes to level. The message treatment is the skillful author's opportunity to harness together the "meanings" and "feeling tones" into a vivid literary experience by making careful choices with regard to code and content. This explains somewhat the isolated message ingredients, but the oral interpreter misses the mark if he does not seek a synthesis of the complex of attitudes which causes the audience to submit itself fully to the imaginative and powerful total effect which is the author's message. It is possible to know a literary piece intimately and still miss the total experience. It would be difficult, if not impossible, to explain satisfactorily this complex of attitudes and the nature of the responses made by reader and audience.

The complex of attitudes can be explained to some degree, however, through a discussion of symbolism. Art achieves its purpose, like all human communication, through symbols and meanings derived from these symbols. Symbols convey meaning on many levels and frequently on many levels simultaneously. The denotative or concrete meaning may be presented on one level, and a transcendant or connotative meaning on another level and both may be communicated at one time, the *complete* meaning resulting from total response. People have the same meanings only to the extent that they have had the same or similar experiences, or are able to anticipate similar experiences. Meaning, then, may be understood as response, and responses to words, phrases, and ideas will always be as individual, varied and complicated as the experiences of the reader or audience.

Symbolism is common to us, but perhaps not significant to us until we realize that total response is possible only when experience and meaning are simultaneous. That is, the complex of attitudes must work as a *gestalt* in forcefully combining all the stimuli which produce involvement and meaning. This multiple-meaning structure is the primary concern of what has been called the New Criticism.[10] These new critics warn against the impression that the meanings of the symbols in a work of literary art can be exhausted. We, as oral interpreters, are in complete agreement with these critics that total response is approached only after an attempt is made to communicate the whole spectrum of stimuli provided by the author and his medium of expression. This requires a unification of knowledge and imagination in vivifying the complex of attitudes and emotions presented by the symbols.

In understanding his art the oral interpreter must realize that the writer chooses word symbols, not only to express facts, but also to convey overtones which transcend literal meaning and lead the reader to a complete and unified experience. The construction of the mosaic by the writer, with its multiple-meaning structure and interlocking symbols, must be understood by the oral interpreter and an attempt made to communicate it. If his communication is effective, the audience can experience as much as their minds and imaginations are capable of, and with a degree of directness found in few other mediums.

SUMMARY

Oral interpretation is a process which can be taught and learned. This chapter began by suggesting a few of the possible "relevant elements" involved in the process. We examined an elaborate but incomplete model of the process, and finally we centered our discussion on a few of the possible problem areas.

Serious scholars and students in the area of oral interpretation would do well to examine their art in light of established communication theory. They must remember, however, that the success or failure of the oral interpretation act is determined by audience response, and this response, like that of the theatre audience, occurs in an aesthetic environment. (See Chapter 6) There is much to be discovered concerning this environment and the successful methods of communicating within its boundaries.

FOOTNOTES

[1]See David K. Berlo, *The Process of Communication* (New York: Holt, Rinehart and Winston, 1960), and Raymond S. Ross, *Speech Communication* (New Jersey: Prentice Hall, Inc., 1965).

[2]Berlo, *op. cit.,* p. 24.

[3]For another model of the oral interpretation process see Smith, Joseph and James Linn, *Skill in Reading Aloud* (New York: Harper and Row, 1960), p. 381.

[4]Max Eastman, "The Art of Enjoying Poetry",*The Meaning in Reading,* edited by J. H. Wise and others. (New York: Harcourt, Brace and Company, 1943), p. 131.

[5]See Charlotte Lee, *Oral Interpretation,* third edition (Boston: Houghton Mifflin Company, 1965), and Otis Aggertt and Elbert Bowen, Communicative Reading, second edition (New York: Macmillan Company, 1962).

[6]Leo Tolstoy, *What Is Art?* (New York: Thomas Y. Crowell and Company, 1899), p. 50.

[7]John T. Marshman, "Art Approach to Reading Aloud", *Quarterly Journal of Speech* (February, 1951), p. 38.

[8]Wallace Bacon and Robert Breen, *Literature as Experience* (New York: McGraw Hill Book Company, 1959), p. 46.

[9]Berlo, *op. cit.,* p. 54.

[10]For comments on Oral Interpretation and the New Criticism see Don Geiger, "Oral Interpretation and the 'New Criticism'," *Quarterly Journal of Speech* (December, 1950), and Anthony Ostroff, "New Criticism and Oral Interpretation,"*Western Speech* (January, 1954).

FURTHER READINGS

BOOKS

Abrams, The Mirror and the Lamp: Romantic Theory and the Critical Tradition. Inc., New York, 1958.

Armstrong, Chloe and Paul D. Brandes, *The Oral Interpretation of Literature.* McGraw-Hill Book Company, New York, 1963.

Auerbach, Erich, *The Mimesis.* Trans. William Tras, Princeton University Press, Princeton, New Jersey, 1953. (1957 paperback)

Bacon,Wallace A. and Robert Breen *Literature as Experience.* McGraw-Hill Book Company, Inc., New York, 1959.

Beebe,Maurice, *Literary Symbolism: An Introduction to the Interpretation of Literature.* Wadsworth Publishing Company, San Francisco, 1960.

Berlo,David K., *The Process of Communication.* Holt, Rinehart and Winston, Inc., New York, 1960.

Blackmur, R. P., *Language as Gesture.* Harcourt, Brace and Company, New York, 1951.

Condon, John C.,*Semantics and Communication.* Macmillan Company, New York, 1966.

Geiger, Don, *The Sound, Sense, and Performance of Literature.* Scott, Forseman Company, Chicago, 1963.

Lewis, C. Day, *The Poet's Way of Knowledge.* Cambridge University Press, New York, 1957.

Miller, Gerald, *Speech Communication: A Behavioral Approach.* Bobbs-Merrill Company, New York, 1966.

Parker, DeWitt, *The Principles of Aesthetics.* 2nd edition. Appleton-Century-Crofts, Inc., New York, 1946.

Ransom, John Crowe, *The New Criticism.* New Directions Press, Norfolk, Connecticut, 1941.

Skinner, B. F., *Verbal Behavior.* Appleton-Century-Crofts, New York, 1957.

Tindall, William York, *The Literary Symbol.* Columbia University Press, New York, 1955. (1958, paperback)

ARTICLES

Feather, N. T., "A Structural Balance Model of Communication Effects", *Psychological Review,* LXXI (July, 1964), pp. 291-314.

Hargis, Donald, "What Is Oral Interpretation?", *Western Speech,* XVI (May, 1951).

Johnson, F. Craig, and George Klare, "General Models of Communication Research: A Survey of the Development of a Decade, *Journal of Communication,* XI (March, 1961).

Chapter II

THE INTERPRETER: THE NATURE OF HIS ART

Jere Veilleux

Much confusion surrounds the nature of the oral interpreter's art. This chapter analyzes some of the misunderstandings and offers suggestions as to oral interpretation's contributions in research and performance.

The oral interpretation process occurs in an aesthetic environment and is certainly one of the oldest of the speech arts. It might be argued, perhaps sophistically, that it is the oldest, that even the arts of rhetoric and of the theatre were preceded by the art of telling tales, the imaginative recital of myths and epics. But oral interpretation is also the most consistently misunderstood of the speech arts. Among even informed students and teachers of speech, basic questions about the purposes, values, techniques, and styles of interpretation are common. In an attempt to resolve some of the confusions about oral interpretation, this chapter will consider the qualitative nature of the interpretative act.

Following Marshall McLuhan's distinctions between "hot" and "cool" media[1] (a "cool" medium is basically one which involves a high degree of participation because it more completely provides the data for its audience), it would be reasonable to argue that oral interpretation is not only the oldest but also the coolest of the speech arts. Interpretation is a form of communication in which the interpreter only "suggests" and the language only "implies," while the audience is charged with the responsibility of conclusion and judgment. As a process of communication, interpretation differs from the other speech media not only in its content (a fact that has been well understood) but also in its basic form: the "act" of interpretation is a qualitatively different act from the act of public speaking or of acting.

Since the Second World War oral interpretative activity has expanded immensely. Beginning with the First Drama Quartet's artistic and financial success, "Don Juan in Hell," the number of professional staged readings has grown so much that at least half a dozen new successful productions are available in the New York area during a given season. Poets are reading their poetry everywhere, and for very good fees indeed. The variety of college and university readers' theatres (or staged interpretations called by other names) is apparent to any observer of the scene. All major speech departments now include a sequence in oral interpretation; some states now include one such course in their teacher certification requirements, not only for teachers of speech, but for teachers of English as well. Finally, oral interpretation is being used more and more as a positive tool in remedial work, especially with troubled or disadvantaged children.

*Portions reprinted from *The Speech Teacher* March, 1967, by permission of the Speech Association of America.

Despite this renascence in oral interpretation or perhaps because of it, one finds confusion about what interpretation is: its nature as a performing art, and its role in relation to such established academic areas as public address, theatre, and speech science. Professional readings are attacked by the critics either because they are not theatrical enough, or if they are theatrical enough, their designation as a reading performance is dismissed as a misnomer. Although the poets get paid, most of them are reading their poetry badly. We have a hundred "readers' theatres" (few of them acoustically designed for interpretation), but no one has seriously attempted to define the form or to pursue its ramifications. And in many speech departments the area of interpretation still plays a relatively minor role; sometimes interpretation courses are even listed under public address, which hardly indicates an understanding of its art. A perennially voiced view is that interpretation is merely a modified form of acting of peripheral value to the student, but hardly an area of any academic depth. Research in interpretation is valued even less; the chairman of one large speech department remarked to me that he simply saw no research possibilities in oral interpretation.

There are, I think, some good reasons for this continuing confusion about oral interpretation. For one thing, the contemporary practice of staging readings, professionsl and amateur, has been developed by its own impetus and with its own entrepreneurs, without any established tradition or theory to support it. The actor and the director can look to a rich theatrical tradition for practical help in training and performance and to any of several schools of thought for a basis in theory. The interpreter and the interpretative director can only gaze back in dismay at the Elocutionists and the Chautauqua. Another reason for the confusion undoubtedly lies in the rebirth of oral interpretation as a literary rather than oratorical art. Interpretation was once, but no longer, the handmaided of rhetoric. The approaches of the new linguists and the continuing insights of the New Critics, both with their recognition of the values in oral expression of the text, have given interpretation a new justification for being in our time: the performance of literature for its own sake.

A more damning reason for the existing confusion about oral interpretation lies with those of us who have taught and written in the area. One can hardly wonder that people believe there is no research to be done in oral interpretation when so blessed little has been done. The number of masters' theses and doctoral dissertations has been abysmally small; the quality and quantity of other research, experimental and historical, hardly compares with similar work done in public address, theatre, or pathology. We do not even publish very useful or complete bibliographies of materials in our field.

Yet I believe, along with many others, that staged reading productions need further theoretical consideration and practical experimentation, that the teaching of interpretation is both a valuable and a necessary activity, and that research into the nature, history, and practice of interpretation is urgently needed. But none of these things can occur if our own confusions continue to relegate interpretation to a minor academic role and to dismiss it as a serious art form.

THE INTERPRETER'S ROLE

Confusion over the present theory and practice of oral interpretation seems to arise out of three basic areas of misunderstanding. The first of these areas can best be illuminated by raising once again the tiresome question of the distinctions between oral interpretation and acting; the confusion here is a result of the seemingly closely analogical techniques of the two disciplines. The second source lies in the nature of the peculiar language of oral interpretation as compared with the more familiar languages of rhetoric and of science. And the third source is the failure to perceive the unique psychology of the audience present in the interpretative situation.

First of all, interpretation vs. acting. No one who has ever taught interpretation has not faced the problem; if the instructor does not raise the question, the student will. "When does interpretation become acting? How does it differ from acting? If interpretation is *not* acting, what is it?"[2]

These are very real questions and, I assure you, difficult ones to answer in either practical or theoretical terms. When one thinks he has an answer, he is soon faced either with a hybrid performance which does not fit his definition at all, or with a surprisingly efficacious example of movement or gesture which demolishes the necessity for definition. Will Geer successfully and delightfully dresses up to impersonate Robert Frost, or Hal Holbrook as Twain, or Emlyn Williams as Dickens. Or the bright student brilliantly "acts out" William Carlos Williams' charming little poem about the cat--moving around an imaginary "jamcloset" and, somehow, dropping with great feline charm into an imaginary "flowerpot." A splendid interpretation!

I would suggest that this question of definition be raised in a somewhat different form. I would insist that oral interpretation be defined on its own terms. The usual question is always: "How does oral interpretation differ from acting?"–not the other way around. Yet, historically, the storyteller undoubtedly came before the actor, who finally then evoked his own theatrical mode for telling the dramatic story. Could we not say that acting is one way of interpreting literature, particularly and necessarily suited to the dramatic form, the play; that reciting a poem or reading a story is another way; that even impersonation and pantomine are others?

The form of a piece of literature necessarily indicates the direction of its performance. All written literature can be read silently, of course. Prose fiction, the novel, for example, is probably intended primarily for the silent reader. But most poets and audiences believe in the power and value of poetry read aloud, to assure its more complete effect. The play, certainly, was meant to be performed by actors on a stage. But these three forms have no absolute structural limits; they shade into one another and so do the possibilities for their performance. While a play, a dramatic form, is intended for its actors, few people would claim that the dramatic monologue, again, a dramatic form, needs an actor's performance. It might enhance "My Last Duchess" to have it performed on a stage with two actors, in costume, with properties and setting. Most readers, however, would probably enjoy the poem just as much through silent reading–or through oral interpretation. Some dramatic forms, the "closet dramas," which perform poorly on the stage and thus are destined for the silent reader, intended so or not, can even be rescued by the oral interpreter.

Even though the form of literature may indicate a direction for its performance, it does not necessarily indicate the only direction. When one hears a poem read aloud by another, he hears it as different from his own silent reading of it. The capable performance of the poem inevitably means a gain, through sound, in the poetic communication itself. A modern short story is not necessarily designed for the ear (though certainly one must "hear" Eudora Welty's stories). But the process of hearing a story is the only way through which we can become aware of the sound of the author's words, an element of language present in any story whether or not by conscious intention. The oral interpretation of either story or poem is also a way of obtaining another perspective, outside ourselves; it is an act of criticism. And the fact is–we enjoy hearing poems and stories perceptively interpreted for us.

The values of interpretation seem to be harder to justify in terms of the performance of a play. Why should an audience hear a play interpreted when it can hear and see the same play acted? Would *King Lear* be as effective in a staged reading as in a fully acted production? Reserving comment on the first question, I would think that the obvious answer to the second question is "All things being equal–No." The full effect of a play is in its theatrical production, if the production is a good one.

But there are vast differences among theatrical productions: a Roman play can be done in period costume, contemporary costume, abstract costume, or no costume. What constitutes theatre in one sense may not be theatre in another; arena and proscenium stages make different plays out of the same drama. The theatre director makes dicisions about staging and lighting and costuming and all the elements of production in the light of his concept of the play's production. The critics and audiences comment on the final product, but no one questions his right to make such decisions, to stage his theatrical production as he sees fit.

The interpreter, too, when he deals with drama, must make production decisions, and as he does so, he must keep in mind the nature of his own medium and refuse to be irrelevantly distracted by apparent analogies with the theatre. For the oral interpreter cannot present a play in its fully staged theatrical form any more than he could conceivably present a novel as a silent reading experience; in both cases, the obvious and usual mode of literary communication is simply not available to him. But the interpreter can still perform the drama in another direction. He can present the play through oral interpretation, thus augmenting the silent and individual literary responses of his audience. His scene is the reading room; his costumes are provided by his listeners.

And to emphasize the aural over the visual is not necessarily a loss. "The auditory field is simultaneous, the visual mode is successive."[3] Interpretation, by neutralizing the visual element of a play, emphasizes the simultaneity of its experience, much as pantomine, by neutralizing the aural element, emphasizes the successiveness of experience. Either mode, through such sensory exclusion, leads us to more particular delights and wisdom.

Just as radio and television excel in the immediacy of their presentation, or as the film excels in its use of the close-up, so the medium of oral interpretation has its own strengths and possibilities. The interpreter, while recognizing the theatrical potential of his dramatic material, simply handles the play in different terms than do the actor and director.

Actually, we might say that only the silent reader of a play sees the truly perfect production; he creates his own perfect imaginary actors and settings as he reads the dialogue. Almost all theatrical productions are less successful than our own imagined ones; thus, the inevitable existence of drama critics. (Of course, our own mental productions are not quite so good as we think they are, but we don't know that.) But nobody would argue, then, that we should not see plays, and the fact remains that we want to, even though the best of productions fall below our expectations in one way or another. Oral interpretation is simply another way, mimetic but not histrionic, with emphasis on the aural rather than the visual, through which dramatic literature can be performed, appreciated, and understood. All things, unfortunately, are not always equal: a good oral interpretation of *King Lear* is a nobler gesture toward both Shakespeare and his audience than a poor theatrical production.

Not only do we need to view oral interpretation as a separate medium and thus define its conventions without reference to its irrelevant resemblances to acting; we must also allow the individual oral interpreter a wider range within which to work. Unfortunately most oral interpreters tend to be indistinguishable from one another; perhaps our textbooks encourage this with their emphases on the primacy of the literature or on the necessity of rigid conventions. Yet actors have personalities despite their being actors. We are untroubled by the existence of different schools of acting (method, British, epic theatre), yet there seems today to be only one school of interpretation. Why can we not allow the interpreter more magnitude in which to develop his own style or to experiment with several styles? Should we be so sure that our contemporary mode of interpretation allows even enough latitude to meet the demands of the more aggressive modern literature?[4]

While the art of the interpreter is different from that of the actor, the interpreter needs no less to experiment with his own craft. Especially does he need to exercise his imagination with the possibilities of movement and gesture. While the focus in interpretation is aural, it is a mistake to think that the audience sees nothing. In fact, I can think of no valid theoretical objection to impersonation as one possible style of interpretation; certainly the Frost, Twain, and Dickens presentations successfully demonstrated its possibilities. We recognize that modes of theatrical production change as they mirror society's changing tastes; the 18th Century's Shakespeare is certainly not ours, and probably neither is the Elizabethan's. I suspect that the fact that impersonation is currently out of vogue, while suggestion is in, is due more to our own tastes in performance than to any cosmic insight into the nature of interpretation.

We cannot excuse bad oral interpretation by calling it either acting or simply reading. The oral interpreter has the responsibility for defining the limits and possibilities of his own medium and for developing his own style of presentation.

THE INTERPRETER'S LANGUAGE

A second source for misunderstanding in oral interpretation is a failure to distinguish the unique character of its language. The type of communication which occurs in the interpretative process is not the same as that which occurs in either the rhetorical process or the scientific process. The language of oral interpretation is primarily emotive rather than discursive or scientific.[5]

The confusion of the role of the oral interpreter with that of the public speaker seems to go far back historically, even though the Aristotelian distinction between rhetoric and poetics has always been clear enough. Certainly the Elocutionists did not clearly isolate the roles of the reader and speaker, nor do most current writers. Perhaps the fact that the public speaker always uses "emotional" appeals, that he can be aided in delivery by the study of oral reading, and that, in past times, he has been taught the art of elocution including reading for the purpose of training him for public speaking--such factors may have muddied the original distinction between the interpreter and the speaker.

Our traditional Western assumption about the public speaker is that his discourse is, or ought to be, firmly grounded in reason. We recognize the role of the imagination in the invention of topics and the employment of metaphor, but its role is ancillary. The speaker attempts to ínform or persuade primarily by presenting logical, well reasoned data supported by sound evidence. While the speaker uses emotional and ethical appeals as he can, his language should rely heavily on well-ordered fact; a metaphor is no substitute for a statistic. At least this is what we teach our students. In fact, the more clarity and logic our discourse has, the better we seem to like it.

The oral interpreter, however, attempts neither to persuade nor to inform. His province is literature, primarily fiction and poetic literature. He may, of course, interpret a speech, or some other nonfictional form, but even then his purpose will differ from the purpose of the original speaker; he will have removed the speech from its historic context and thus, in a sense, made it literature rather than rhetoric. And insofar as the interpreter's province is literature, the language with which he must deal is emotive rather than logical. Literature, while it does, of course, contain facts and arguments, speaks primarily the language of emotion. Literature speaks with the language of implication rather than statement, of question rather than answer, of symbol rather than reality. When the drama, the story, and the poem do have discursive features, they are seldom tied to specific aims--the communication of necessary information or the appeal to specific belief-- but are informative or persuasive only in the sense of the author's expression of a *Weltanschauung* (ideology).

Thus the interpreter is concerned with the communication of emotional meanings rather than discursive meanings. So we cannot judge oral interpretation by rhetorical standards; since its message is different, so are its techniques. The ethos of the oral interpreter, for instance, is relatively unimportant. Nor should we expect the same effects in the interpretative situation as in the public address situation. The meanings conveyed through oral interpretation are at the same time deeper and vaguer than those conveyed through public address. The Interpreter may at times mystify, anger, or shock his audience—surely not the conventional aims of the public speaker.

The effective interpreter fortunately is well equipped to express the emotive language of literature, at times even better equipped than the author of the literature himself. For the interpreter has a formidable weapon—inflection. A given word on the printed page ("but," for example) has its grammatical and syntactical meaning, but the interpreter's possible inflections of that word to suggest its emotional content are perhaps infinite.[6]

What we need to do, both as members of the audience and as interpreters, is to accept the oral expression of emotional meaning as a thoroughly valid mode of communication. The oral interpreter is as fully an artist as the actor and as good a citizen as the speaker; emotive language is indeed the only language with which to express certain thoughts. While interpretation can be put to more practical purposes, its essential value is as an imaginative art.

THE INTERPRETER'S AUDIENCE

Related to the problem of recognizing the emotive language distinctive to interpretation is the problem of recognizing the peculiar phenomenon of the audience in the interpretative situation. Because of vague or false expectations of what does or should occur in the oral interpreter's audience, critics and audiences alike find themselves liking or disliking a reading performance without being able to say quite why.

All students of speech and theatre are aware of the nature of an audience–they know that a group of disparate individuals takes on a corporate identity, becomes an "audience," in response to what they see and hear. As an audience the group becomes something more than the sum of its individuals, yet each member retains at the same time his individuality. The response of laughter, for instance, is heightened by a large audience; the individual tends to laugh more often and louder than he would ordinarily.

The audience phenomenon functions in oral interpretation in a particular way. If we contrast the interpretative situation with the two most common speech live audience situations (theatre and public address), we can see two distinct differences. First, as we noted previously, the interpretative experience is primarily auditory; the visual spectacle of the theatre is lacking. Conventionally, this is reinforced by the lack of forced visual focus in the fully lighted reading room. Second, the interpreter's material is usually neither original nor created for any special purpose, need, or occasion, as is the usual case with public address. Indeed, the material for interpretation is very often familiar to the audience; the literature is re-created by the interpreter for its own sake.

These two factors, the focus on the auditory and the intrinsic appeal of the literature, create an unusual effect. First of all, the spectator's mind tends to be more actively engaged than it would be in the theatre. The listener, with the interpreter's help, must himself re-create the setting, costumes, and lighting of the play, attend more closely than the silent reader to the narrative of the story, and struggle with the linguistic ambiguities of the spoken poem. While the language of interpretation is emotive, the process of interpretation involves a high degree of internal visualization and critical reflection for the audience. When the interpretation is successful, since the appeal is directed primarily to the auditory sense and since literature often provides ambiguous information, the members of the audience are forced to participate with active imaginations in the interpretative process.

Secondly, the response of the audience in interpretation tends to be more homogeneous than in public address. An audience recognizes good interpretation, especially with familiar material, in much the way the opera buff knows when to shout "Bravo!" But since the focus in good interpretation is always on the literature rather than on the interpreter, the audience response, unlike that of the opera buff, cannot be entirely directed to the virtuosity of the performance. Nor can it really be a response to the literature when, at times, the audience is already familiar with what is read. To what then is the audience responding?

The closest analogy to the interpretative audience is that of the symphonic audience. There, too, the emphasis is auditory, the language emotive, the material often familiar; they re-create their own patterns of imaginative response. Now at a symphony there may be disagreement among the audience about the way a work is conducted, about the techniques of various members of the orchestra, or about the quality of the given work itself. But there is seldom disagreement about the "meaning" of the work itself since the performance of music does not allow for easy translation into discursive terms. The audience's response to a "good" symphonic performance is necessarily a function of their individual subjective reactions (what the music "means" to them personally), though they may all applaud at the same time.

And this is the curious phenomenon which also presents itself in interpretation. A group of very diverse individuals, who have strong personal feelings, prejudices, and opinions, who should disagree about almost everything, often will find themselves, upon hearing a poem, play, or story well interpreted, in unanimous agreement not just about the quality of the interpretation, but also about the values projected by the literature.

But then ask them to discuss or explain what the work means! And soon they will begin to argue about the author's intention, tell irrelevant anecdotes from their own experience, and dispute the fact that the material holds any universal meaning at all. In effect, their responses as an audience were primarily to their own feelings rather than to the interpreter or to the literature. They responded individually and subjectively to the universal and affirmative feelings which the skill of author and interpreter had aroused once again in their own hearts. At least in part, they were applauding themselves.

We have returned here to the distinction between emotive and discursive language. In good interpretation, as in good literature, the importance of man's ephemeral disputations is set in the larger context of man's universal hopes, fears, and aspirations. Thus, the experience of the literature itself tends to result in apparent agreement, while the experience of the discussion of that literature tends to lead to dissension.

The nature of the audience, then, as it responds to oral interpretation, is different from that of other audiences. Its imagination is necessarily more active than in the theatre, and its response is likely to be more harmonious than in the forum. Perhaps the audience's active commitment to understanding the literature tends to reinforce the probability of its common response.

And we should realize that both interpreter and audience seem to want the experience of oral interpretation. Storytelling is probably the hardiest of man's traditions. Ages of the written word do not seem to diminish seriously man's desire to tell stories aloud, nor his need to hear them told. Marshall McLuhan has commented on such a need which is more than just aural: "Radio and gramophone and tape recorder gave us back the poet's voice as an important dimension of the poetic experience. Words became a kind of painting with light, again. But TV, with its deep-participation mode, caused young poets suddenly to present their poems in cafes, in public parks, anywhere. After TV, they suddenly felt the need for personal contact with their public."[7] The telling of written literature not only brings it to life, but makes of it a social event.

THE FUTURE OF INTERPRETATION

What, then, should be the role of oral interpretation in the speech curriculum? What are the legitimate possibilities for research in oral interpretation? What unique functions might oral interpretation fulfill as a performing art?

Despite C. P. Snow, we must recognize some significant differences between science and poetry. Oral interpretation is at the far end of the speech spectrum, speech pathology and audiology at the other. The aims and techniques of the two disciplines are far apart; they can complement the education of our students, but they cannot be taught or learned in the same way, nor should they be. As Anthony Hillbruner suggests, oral interpretation is the "aesthetic dimension" of speech study, that without interpretation the speech curriculum is a "body without a soul."[8]

Oral interpretation is essentially a liberal art: a speech approach to the understanding and appreciation of literature. It is a valuable adjunct to all areas in the speech curriculum. As such, it provides a humanizing antidote for the speech scientist and a reminder of the values of literature for the student of public address. It is not theatre, and does not want to be, but it can help the would-be actor to test himself through work in another medium.

But oral interpretation is also a valuable and valid performing art, a serious study in itself; it is not merely a method of training the actor, the speaker, or the clinician. We must take seriously the end effect of interpretation, public performance if we expect our students to take any part of interpretation seriously. To deny the interpreter's successful performance before an audience as the goal of interpretation is to cast doubt on the efficacy of its techniques in other ways. If we are not to perform the literature, after all our struggle and preparation, what then are we to do with it?

Research in oral interpretation has been much neglected. Anthropologists have been concerned with the storytelling tradition throughout the world, but not students of interpretation. Historians have been concerned with the jongleurs and the troubadours, but not students of interpretation. There is a need not only for historical research, but for sound experimental studies in the nature of the audience phenomenon, the effectiveness of various types of movement and gesture, and the principles of staged reading presentations. Modern problems in interpretation theory and practice will be solved only in the light of knowledge from such research.

There are two distinct contributions which oral interpretation can make in the area of performance. The first is the performance of that literature which existed first of all as oral literature and is now known to readers and students only in its later written translations. The Greek epics, *The Iliad* and *The Odyssey,* particularly could profit from the vitality of adaptation for interpretative performance. The second significant area in which interpretation can make such a contribution is in the performance of unpublished, avant-garde works. Publication too often means conservatism; when an author has been "accepted," the possibility of written form follows. Interpretation can serve both artist and audience through the performance of new, unpublished, indeed exciting or even shocking, works.

"We must have a more profound, comprehensive, and accurate discernment of the good and evil involved in the social developments of our time. This must be created in the minds of men by the kind of speech which communicates from one to another the deepest discernment of value each has attained," Henry Nelson Wieman wrote in a *Quarterly Journal of Speech* article entitled "Speech in the Existential Situation."[9] Just as the existentialists argue that the best way to philosophize is through literature, so the oral interpreter believes that the best way to experience literature is through performance. Performance, because those deeper discernments of value need more than a private hearing and oral interpretation is the only speech art which can communicate some of them.

FOOTNOTES

[1]Marshall McLuhan, *Understanding Media: The Extensions of Man* (New York: McGraw-Hill Book Co., 1965), pp. 22-32.

2One might think that Gertrude Johnson's excellent collection of essays, *Studies in the Art of Interpretation* (New York: Appleton-Century-Crofts, Inc., 1940), most of which dealt with this problem, would have been the last word. But the problem is present a quarter of a century later; see Philip Boyd Stevens' perceptive "Acting and Interpretation: The Reader Faces the Contest," *Speech Teacher,* XIV (March 1965), pp. 116-122.

3Marshall McLuhan, *The Gutenberg Galaxy* (Toronto, Canada: University of Toronto Press, 1962), p. 111.

4Such articles as: Hugh Dickinson, "Readers or Rhapsodes?" *Quarterly Journal of Speech,* XLV (October 1959), pp. 258-263, and Wallace A. Bacon, "The Dangerous Shores: From Elocution to Interpretation," *Quarterly Journal of Speech,* XLVI (April 1960), pp. 148-152, distinguish well the traditional range for the interpreter's art. But are there perhaps possibilities of style beyond these limits, even "absurd" styles?

5Probably it is obvious that the language of interpretation is not scientific; it is less obvious, and just as important, to realize that it is not discursive. David W. Thompson and Virginia Fredricks, *Oral Interpretation of Fiction* (Minneapolis: Burgess Publishing Co., 1964), p. 1, put it concisely: "It is the difference between Aristotle's *Rhetoric* and his *Poetics,* ...Rhetoric, debate, public speaking and discussion usually make use of propositional, discursive language. Interpretation, on the other hand, like the literature it deals with, uses intuitive, evocative, emotive speech."

6See Marshall McLuhan, *The Gutenberg Galaxy,* pp. 231-233.

7Marshall McLuhan, *Understanding Media: The Extensions of Man,* p. 53.

8Anthony Hillbruner, "Interpretation, Aesthetics, and the Speech Curriculum," *VIII (January 959), p. 23.*

9Henry Nelson Wieman, "Speech in the Existential Situation," *Quarterly Journal of Speech,* XLVII (April 1961), p. 157.

FURTHER READINGS

BOOKS

Beloof, Robert, *The Performing Voice in Literature.* Little, Brown and Company. Boston, 1966.
Sloan, Thomas O., ed., *The Oral Study of Literature.* Random House, Inc., New York, 1966

ARTICLES

Brooks, Keith and Sr. I. Marie Wulftange, "Listener Response to Oral Interpretation," *Speech Monographs,* XXXI (March, 1964), pp. 73-79.
Geiger, Don, "Oral Interpretation and the 'New Criticism,'" *Quarterly Journal of Speech,* XXXVI (December, 1950), pp. 508-513.
Marcoux, J. Paul, "Current Trends in Literary Analysis for Oral Interpretation: An Overview," *Speech Teacher,* XIV (November, 1966) pp. 324-327.
Ness, Ordean G., "The Value of Oral Interpretation to the Student in General Speech," *Speech Teacher,* V (September, 1956), pp. 208-213.
Rarig, Frank M., "Some Elementary Contributions of Aesthetics to Interpretative Speech," *Quarterly Journal of Speech,* XXVI (December, 1940), pp. 527-539.
Reitz, Mathias, "The Application of Selected Dramatic Theories of Stanislavski as a Solution to Disunity in Readers' Theatre," *Speech Teacher,* XV (September, 1966), pp. 191-196.
Sloan, Thomas O., "Restoration of Rhetoric to Literary Study," *Speech Teacher,* XVI (March, 1967), pp. 91-97.
Thompson, David W., "Interpretative Reading as Symbolic Action," *Quarterly Journal of Speech,* XLII, (December, 1956), pp. 389-397.

Chapter III

THE WRITER: POET'S THOUGHTS ON ORAL INTERPRETATION

M. Blair Hart

This chapter turns our attention from the oral interpreter to the creative writer, specifically the poet, and evaluates his comments and performances in the area of oral interpretation.

Poets are not outspoken on the interpreter's art; one must search to find significant comment. Nor have poets established among themselves a common agreement on the proper way to read poetry. A few have claimed no interest in the public reaction and write only for the "inner ear," while others prefer the recorded voice to separate the "sound of poetry from the distraction of performance." In contrast, a number of poets have established considerable reputation as readers of their own poetry–although their techniques differ widely. The American poet, Thomas Hornsby Ferril, believes that any skilled interpreter can read his poetry successfully. Others feel that actors or oral interpreters cannot read poetry as they want to hear it read.

Writers are aware, however, of the poetic values of sound, for surely the poet must have an ear for the play and pattern of sound that his choice of words create; yet the memory of sound, dancing through poetic images, is a different art from the interpreter's task of creating those sounds for a listening audience. Dylan Thomas, reflecting on his own reading, phrased the question that has been the center of many academic discussions: "Reading one's own poems aloud is letting the cat out of the bag. . . Does the cat snarl or mew the better when its original owner--or father, even, the tom poet--lets it out of the bag, than when another does, who never put it in?"[1]

He was, at that time, aware of the problems he encountered in trying to awaken his own memory to the original impulses which had shaped the poems he had chosen to read aloud to an audience. He suspected that the attempt to dredge up those impulses from the moment of poetic birth led the poet to a kind of melodramatic reading "making a simple phrase break with the fear or throb with the terrors from which he deludes himself the phrase has been born." Yet Thomas did become one of the outstanding poet readers of his time. He succeeded remarkably well in "deeping the inner meaning" of his poetic lines, especially those which are direct in statement and essentially dramatic.

That Thomas found it more difficult to gain equal clarity in poems packed with complex and often conflicting images should not surprise the student of oral interpretation. How much complexity can be caught and digested by the ear alone when linked with the tempo of continuous utterance--how much should be attempted--is a matter of judgment that faces every public reader. Although Thomas, as a reader, was sometimes compared to Charles Laughton (especially in physical appearance and the rich quality of voice), Laughton was the more skillful reader and the more cautious in the selections he chose to read for the public.

POETS, PERFORMERS, AND PERSONALITIES

There is a closely related aspect of oral interpretation which I shall not attempt to discuss, except to mention the point briefly: the oral reading of poetry cannot be divorced completely from the personality of the reader--whether he be poet or interpreter. Amy Lowell gave a fire and significance to her reading that later critics could not find in many of the poems she had read. When commenting on her own success as a reader, she pointed out that she had come from a family of public speakers. In short, a strong personality and skillful reader can add qualities beyond those apparent on the printed page in much the same manner that a dull personality and an unskilled reader can destroy what an imaginative poet has created.

In a richly descriptive article entitled "The Poet as Player," (published in 1957, unfortunately now out of print), Gerald Weales divided the poet readers he had heard into three groups: the performer, the personality, and the public speaker.[2] For Mr. Weales, and many others no doubt, Dame Edith Sitwell stood as the queen of the poet-performers. She created a stage personality and manner of delivery that was as interesting as the poetry she read. The delivery was part of the performance. Dylan Thomas, Ogden Nash, W. H. Auden, and e. e. cummings were also among the performers--each with a particular way of relating himself to the audience-as-listener. The performance of e. e. cummings was most carefully aimed at the mind; that most dramatic.

Gerald Weales has placed Archibald Macleish and Stephen Spender among the public speakers because their elaborate intro-ductions and careful attention to chronological order "makes one feel he should be taking notes," even though the occasion leaned toward pleasure rather than education. "If the performer delights the eye and ear, and the public speaker the mind," Weales observed, "the personality must depend on his appeal to the heart." Anyone who has heard Robert Frost would agree he would be placed among the poet-personalities. The kindly wisdom of his verse, the bush brows, the warm simplicity in addressing an audience, seemed to make him every listener's Uncle Bob. Other poets that Mr. Weales has placed among the personalities are: Marianne Moore, Wallace Stephens, T. S. Eliot, and William Carlos Williams. I would have placed the Irish poet, James Stephens, in the same category, for his charm as a reader sprang not from a distinctive stage appearance nor a scholarly manner, but from a twinkling wit that captivated the heart while it infrormed the mind.

Although it may have little bearing on the proper way to read poetry, Mr. Weales observed that the performer nearly always drew the largest crowds to the recital hall.

PERIODS AND POINTS OF VIEW

To appreciate differences in the point of view on reading poetry, it is helpful to observe the "poetic climate" in which different artists have spoken about oral interpretation. For instance, a considerable number of our best known poets were born before the turn of this century and were producing mature works well before 1920. Robinson, Lowell, Frost, Sandburg, Masefield, Stevens, Lindsay, Pound, Sitwell, Eliot, Millay, Macleish, e. e. cummings, and Benet belong in this group. Many of these poets were familiar with the demands of public performance, and American poets were familiar with the Lyceum, Chautauqua, and Redpath circuits.

But literary periods overlap; the new may be half-grown before the public becomes aware of significant change. During the 30's and 40's poetic behavior was less in demand, and observers have referred to the "silent" generation of poets. The literary attitude turned inward to a meticulous study of the poetic structure—to abstraction, symbolic behavior, and a wide range of experimentation in poetic forms no longer bound by traditional demands for direct communication. Louis Simpson, poet and critic attuned to this period, and defending the poets against public criticism of being overly concerned with technique, wrote in 1957, "What matters surely is not the life of the poet but the life of the poem"[3] Richard Wilbur, born in 1921 and a Pulitzer Prize winner in 1957, observed that "much of the modern poetry is too complex to be fully appreciated at a single hearing" and that "few of the contemporary poets are disciplined in the art of oral presentation.[4]

During this period a larger number of poets were joining college and university faculties as one means of providing an income while they continued writing. But the oral interpretation of literature, too long neglected by English departments, had been taken over by the speech and drama departments, as part of the rapidly growing Speech Association of America. Thus, in the large, poets were divorced from the arena of public performance.

The young poets seeking recognition in the 1960's have again turned to vigorous acclaim of oral poetry. Their market place is no longer the public lecture halls of the 20's, but rather the coffee houses, campus student gatherings, the street corner, and private homes. To these young people, poetry is oral-aural, to be heard as a social force must be heard. It is not the poetry taught in the college classroom. It has its own system of values; its rhythms are the rhythms of the 60's.

POETS AS READERS

Few poets have claimed to be the perfect interpreters of their own creations, yet a surprising number of the poets from 1940-1960 have said that actors and trained oral interpreters cannot read their poems as they (the poets) want them read. Among these are such well-known poets as Robert Fitzgerald, Kenneth Rexroth, Richard Wilbur, Philip Booth, Louise Bogan, and Marianne Moore. This voice of dissent has been studied only tangentially and by a limited number of writers. One of the more revealing studies of poets as readers was made by Judith Edworthy Wray in 1961.[5] She concluded that five outstanding readers of the 20th century--Lindsay, Lowell, Sandburg, Frost, and Thomas--demonstrated "more highly developed patterns of inflection (both conversational and incantatory) and more variety in pacing" than was found among seventeen American poets of lesser reputation. Her observation that poets tend "to read slowly and place greater emphasis on meter to the exclusion of other poetic devices" is reflected in the bits of advice that poets have given: read slowly, articulate clearly, read for the sense, follow the meter, speak in a level or monotone conversation. My own memory of Louise Bogan's reading fits the description. She read with flawless articulation, deliberate pacing, and without personal involvement--so that a series of poems with interesting variety of content soon became indistinguishable, covered with a blanket of sameness. I went away feeling that Miss Bogan had wanted us to observe the neatness of the phrasing, the choice of the right word, and the meter on which the poems were built.

By no means all American poets would subscribe to such tight-reigned reading of their poetry, for poets are as varied as people. But to face the issues squarely, I think we must recognize the fact that many contemporary poets feel that the theatre-trained reader has an over-powering urge to turn poetry into "dramatic prose." Even the Welsh poet Dylan Thomas (who was also a playwright), was accused of distortion in reading his lyrics "not as though they were poems full of song, but as though they were dramatic speeches straight out of a play. . ."[6] Poet John Ciardi, because of his continued writing as a critic and explicator of poetic form, has been one of the most vocal on the subject of oral interpretation of poetry. In 1957, Ciardi wrote in *Saturday Review,* "There are in fact few actors who can be trusted to read a poem. Too few have the right sense of restraint and inner echo that makes the poem speak most fully from its silences."[7] Two years later he added, "My general feeling (here subject to revision) has always been that actors simply do not know enough about the kind of performance a poem is."[8] At this time he was emphasizing the need for greater attention to "line end values," to "rhythm punctuation," and to the "thrust and counter-thrust of the total poetic structure." In a review published the following year he noted the flatness of Robert Lowell's reading, but praised his fidelity to cadence and breath groups in which the poems were written.

In a 1961 review of George Starbuck's reading, Ciardi observes that "he reads his own poems in an immediately engaging voice, with a sure sense of their movement, without assertion, and yet with an ever-sensitive engagement of his material and mood."[9] This feel for reading a poem "with-out assertion"—or as some have put it, "let the poem speak for itself"—is perhaps one of the major differences between the attitude of a number of poets who are not public readers by training and the attitude of actors and interpreters who work directly with public audiences. The importance of this difference may have crept into Mr. Ciardi's mind, for in 1962, Beverly Whitaker quoted from correspondence with John Ciardi in which he says quite frankly, "I tend to underplay the reading of my serious poems. . . I hope to learn to say them as I hear them."[10]

Robert Frost, three-time winner of the Pulitzer Prize for poetry, read his poetry in a conversational tone—without strong assertion. He never recited or dramatized his poems, but "said" them, as Louis Untermeyer has noted in *The Letters of Robert Frost.*[11] Yet such a remark can be deceptively misleading, for behind the saying of his poems lay the quiet strength and deep convictions of the man which made it possible for him to "touch lightly those things which were to him also precious," and to convey that depth of conviction to an audience without dramatic assertion. Young readers seldom have the depth of conviction to feel certain that "incidental happenings can be raised to universal significance," or that "the common speech is always giving off. . . the special vocabulary of poetry." Frost read without strong assertion, it seems, because those thoughts expressed in poetic form were, to him, inevitable.

INCANTATION OR CHANT

A word of special attention should be given to the incantation or chant, for it is a vocal technique unfamiliar to college students today. Edgar Allen Poe undoubtedly made strong use of the intoned or incantory style in his highly popular reading of "The Raven" and other poems designed to impress a single mood upon his listeners.[12] It is also evident that Poe possessed an unusually rich and melodious voice; powerful, and used with perfect control. He knew how to build and sustain a mood within the narrow range of pitch inflections that the incantation demands.

Vachel Lindsey was particularly fond of the chant, and on occasion included marginal notes to help the reader grasp his intended tonal effects. A number of people have observed that T. S. Eliot's "dry voice of doom" was particularly effective in reading certain poems. Of the more recent poets, John Frederick Nims, John Ciardi, and Kenneth Rexroth seem to prefer the incantatory coloring to more direct interpretation. It has always seemed to me that the chant or incantation, to be effective, demands a subtle control of other dynamics, combined with the right voice quality, and driven by an inner energy that is more than passive. Some of our contemporary poets who prefer incantation lack the voice and inner dynamics to make the chant effective.

There is also a kind of reading that leans heavily toward song. If one has heard the voice of Carl Sandburg in conversation, in ballad singing, and in the reading of his own poetry, he will recall an unaffected command of tonal effects approaching music. Sandburg's feeling for the "retard" and the "half-pause" spring naturally from his deep, deep sympathies, and from his personal strength—a combination of qualities which one must surely feel in his writing of the Lincoln biography. One is forced to ponder whether Sandburg's techniques for creating music from spoken words can be separated, neatly, from the personality of the man himself.

The World of Carl Sandburg[13] is one of the few attempts to create a major professional program based on the works of a single poet. If he has not already done so, the student of oral interpretation will find interest in the selection, arrangement, and staging--under the direction of Norman Corwin--with comments on cutting and additions which mark some of the differences between public performance and the more intimate reading of poetry. One will also feel the difference between this "performance of poetry" and what Sandburg himself would have done had he read these poems to an audience.

Within my own experience I was delighted and intrigued on first reading the poems of Richard Wilbur, published under the title *Things of This World.* There was subtlety and suggestion and a wonderful flow of rhythms; and many that were too complex in imagery and reference to attempt in a public reading. I found myself coming back to them again and again in an effort to capture their beauty in vocal patterns. I was anxious to hear a recording of Wilbur reading his own poetry. I did, and I was disappointed. It was not the personality, not the oral patterns of sound I had imagined. Had I been years younger and less experienced, I may have tried to imitate his tonal patterns. *That* I would not do. It was considerably later that I read Wilbur's own statement, published in *Mid-Century American Poets,* edited by John Ciardi.14 In a personal letter to Ciardi, Wilbur had made the observation that "with several striking exceptions, our poets (myself included) read in such a way as to convince their audiences hat 'heard melodies are sweet, but those unheard, are sweeter.'" Confidence in myself, and in Wilbur, was restored--especially when I heard him saying to Ciardi that "I want the sounds of my poetry to be heard," and later, "if poets are going to be public readers they should study recitation." I should like to meet Richard Wilbur in person for I am convinced that a poetic spirit so rich as the one recorded in his writing would show through more clearly if one could hear him reading his own poetry rather than listening to a recording--or better yet, hear him talking about his writing experiences.

THE AUDIENCE CONSIDERATION

This brings me to a more recent comment, made by John Ciardi, recorded in the unpublished thesis by Beverly Whitaker. When questioned about his preference for "live performance" in reading as opposed to recording, Ciardi admitted some preference for the *recording* since it gave him sounds of poetry without the distractions of a "performance" of poetry.15 This point illustrates, I suspect, a fundamental difference between the professional writer's interest in sound and that of the oral interpreter who must be concerned with the response of non-professional listeners.

Perhaps I can illustrate the point in another way. I recall a delightful dinner-conversation with an accomplished musician and his wife. We were discussing the enjoyment of music. The professor of organ music admitted that his enjoyment in listening sprang from following the intricate structure of the piece; his wife (a registered nurse by profession) responded in a quite different way. Her enjoyment sprang from the suggestion, the implication, the manner in which the play of sounds directed her imagination to "remembered experiences" and new associations. She was not concerned, as she put it, "with the technical know-how of the composer."

One should not omit in a discussion which touches on the reader and his audience an invitation to hear the recording labeled *"ANTIWORLDS the poetry of ANDREI VOZNESENSKY."*[16] The recording is a series of relatively short poems read first by Voznesensky in his native Russian; each selection is followed immediately by an English translation read by one of four American poets: W. H. Auden, Stanley Kunitz, William Jay Smith, and Richard Wilbur.

Voznesensky has become a national literary figure and something of a hero in his native land. He reads with the full range and intensity of an actor playing the role he loves best; the poetry engulfs the poet. His delight in the endless suggestiveness of words, the range and play of sound, the control of time, and subtle emphasis, is balanced by the unmistakable diction in his native language. By comparison, the American poets seem academic and a trifle dull. The wide differences between the spoken poetry of Andrei Voznesensky and the four Americans hinge on differences in vocal technique and on the poet's attitude toward his audience—variables which are never recorded in the printed poems. Voznesensky reads with depth of passion, for listeners who want to be moved by his poetry.

THE NEW POETRY

While the past thirty years has shown a considerable gap between the established poets and the larger public audience, there was, during this time, a new poetic movement being born. Ezra Pound's protest against artificiality in poetry (and a few other voices) provided inspiration for the emerging poets. William Carlos Williams, followed by Charles Olson and Louis Zukofsky exalted new forms, plain talk, objective subject matter, and lines measured by the rhythm of speech itself. Charles Olson's essay "Projective Verse,"

Pound's "A Retrospect," and similar expressions became rallying points for a kind of bardic free verse bristling with energy, frank language, and poetry reading in the coffee houses where the young and often unpublished poets could be heard. The resurgence of the little poetry magazines, where chaff and quality are freely mingled, underscored the movement, vigorous and romantic in its optimism and energy, and typically 1960 in its mode.

Gary Snyder, a leader of poetic quality among the dozens of young poets drawn to the San Francisco area, asserts that "poets now consider 'reading' to be *the* mode of existence of a poem--just as a play's mode of existence is the performance, not the printed text. . . A poetry deliberately oral has structures now emerging which are different from the conventional 'literary' poetry of line and stanza blocks. A working poet has to learn to breathe from the belly and look and talk straight. No line-break, line drop, or indent, on the printed page is valid if it cannot be meaningfully presented in oral delivery."[17]

To a question concerning his preference for recordings, Gary Snyder gave this reply: "The poem as heard in the voice–from the body–of the man who made it is the best. Second best a reader. Third best a tape or record. Fourth best to read it to yourself aloud. Fifth, silent reading."

Perhaps Gene Fowler typifies the younger group who is learning the craft of poetry on the wing. A leader in the coffee house readings at The Blue Unicorn in 1964, and intimately acquainted with gatherings of every kind from the street corner to the art festival, young Fowler says that "the two forms, the written and the spoken, are so interlocked that I cannot really isolate them any more. A poem that reads wrong when I read it to an audience usually will have bothered me visually on the page."[18] But like numerous poets of an earlier generation, Gene Fowler adds, "I have never heard an actor, even the very fine actors, read a poem in a way that is satisfying to me as a poet. I prefer a straightforward reading. The 'expressions' should come from the poet's re-experiencing of the poem or reaction to the poem and should be as natural as his usual unconscious physical participation in his conversational speech. Genuine facial and bodily expression do, I feel, contribute to the delivery of the poem. Deliberate dramatics detract from the poem, except in very special instances." To Fowler, this spirit of the new generation of poets--the modernity–"isn't in technical procedures or in violation of taboos or in the latest hipness; it's in *tone, rhythm, sound, feel.* . . they are writing out of today with today's feeling and tempo. . . even if it is about swans and thickets."

Every period has its own central concern and its variations. The

"new poetry" is no exception. Robert Duncan insists that his
primary reference is "neither to speech nor to dramatic art but to
music. . . Structure is melodic. . . In the same way 'content' is
melodic: the content of any poem not being the expression of some
thing I want to say but the development of or departure from
elements in the opening statement (which may, in a few cases, be
postponed in the final composition). All constructs--phrasing, stanza,
articulation of the line--are notations for the sounding of the poem. .
. I have in mind always the voice reading aloud obedient to the 'inner
ear' and *never to effects upon the audience. . .* Thus, a singer like
Peter Pears does poetry justice, where actors like Maurice Evans or
Sir Ralph Richardson destroy in their expression the inner measures
and sequences of sound." [19]
     Robert Duncan's concern for the music of poetry parallels
Ciardi's concern for the "inner workings" of poetic structure--of
which, they claim, the actor and oral interpreter know far too little
to be effective readers of poetry. This is, I suspect, the essence of the
poets' thoughts on oral interpretation.

CONCLUSION

     As I write these concluding remarks, I have recently come from
a theatrically staged reading of his own work by the young poet
Edsel Ford. [20] Reading for an audience in-the-round, from four
stands strategically placed to add variety and with light control to
mark transitions and provide time for reflection between key
sections of his program, young Ford carried the solo performance.
Modest and poised, without introductions but carefully planned
sequences, Mr. Ford announced the title of a poem, and then with
meticulous attention to clarity of phrasing and emphasis--unhurried,
but with a sure sense of timing--read with the warmth of remembered
experiences. His reading, like his poetry, is disciplined by form, but
never a slave to form. Rhythms and meter pace the reading and
establish mood his serious poems but never assert themselves, nor
detract from the reader's concentration on the essential experience
of his poetry. For contrast, the obvious play of sounds, the
juxtoposition of ironic images, the quick rhyme and subtle inflections in reading, heighten the humor of his lighter verse.
     I would judge that Edsel Ford reads for a public in the way that
most poets imagine poetry should be read: with the authority of
poetic structure as his guide, with a desire to share creative
experience, and with full awareness of the difference between seeing

and hearing a poem. In his reading Edsel Ford achieves a clear distinction between poetry and conversation on the one hand, and between poetry and dramatization on the other. To him, poetry is a unique form of utterance which communicates while it crystalizes and refines personal experience.

FOOTNOTES

[1]Dylan Thomas, *Quite Early One Morning* (New Directions, 1954), p. 171.

[2]*New World Writing* (No. 11 MD 196 Mentor Book, May, 1957), Gerald Weals, "The Poet as Player."

[3]*Ibid.,* Kenneth Rexroth, "The Art of the Beat Generation."

[4]John Ciardi, *How Does A Poem Mean* (Houghton Mifflin Company, Boston, The Riverside Press, 1960).

[5]Judith Edworthy Wray, (Ph. D. Dissertation), Theories and Methods of Representative Contemporary Poets as Readers of Their Own Poetry" (Unive sity of Wisconsin, 1961).

[6]Gilbert Highet, *The Power of Poetry* (Oxford University Press, 1960), p. 155.

[7]Saturday Review (XL, November 23, 1957), p. 32.

[8]Saturday Review (XLII, May 30 1959), "Actors as Readers", p. 39.

[9]Saturday Review (XLIV, May 13, 1961), p. 58.

[10]Beverly Whitaker, (M. A. Thesis), "John Ciardi: A Poet-Critic on Oral Reading" (Louisiana State University, 1961).

[11]Louis Untermeyer, *The Letters of Robert Frost* (Holt, Rinehart & Winston, 1963).

[12]Southern Speech Journal (XXVIII No. 2, Winter, 1962) John W. Gray, "The Public Reading of Edgar Allen Poe".

[13]Norman Corwin,(Ed),*The World of Carl Sandburg* (Harcourt, Brace & World, Inc., 1961).

[14]John Ciardi (Ed)., *Mid-Century American Poets* (Twayne Publishers, Inc., 1950).

[15]*Op. Cit.* Whitaker, Abstracted from personal correspondence with Ciardi.

[16]Recording: *Antiworlds The Poetry of Andrei Voznesensky* (Columbia OL 6590).

[17]From personal correspondence with Gary Snyder (October 10, 1966).

[18]From personal correspondence with Gary Snyder (September 15, 1966).

[19]From personal correspondence with Robert Duncan (September 15, 1966).

[20]Sponsored by the Fort Smith Little Theatre (Ark.); produced under the direction of Ron Watson.

FURTHER READINGS

BOOKS

Boynton, Percy H., *Some Contemporary Americans.* University of Chicago Press, 1924.

Brenner, Rica, *Ten Modern Poets.* Harcourt, Brace & World, Inc., New York, 1920.

Geiger, Don, *The Sound, Sense, and Performance of Literature.* Scott, Forseman, Chicago, 1963.

Hillyer, Robert, *First Principles of Verse.* The Writer, Inc., 1938.

Lowell, Amy, *Poetry and Poets.* Houghton Mifflin Company, Boston, 1930.
MacLeish, Archibald, *Poetry as Experience.* The Riverside Press, 1960.
Norman, Charles, *The Magic-Maker E. E. Cummings.* The Macmillan Company, 1958.

THESES & DISSERTATIONS

Blodgett, Betty, (M. A. Thesis), "A Study of Dylan Thomas' Public Reading, His Poetic Theory as it Relates to Oral Interpretation.", Auburn University, (1966)..
Cole, Elizabeth Jane, (M. A. Thesis), "The Sound of Poetry: Two Parallels.", University of Mississippi. (1965).
Kuykendall, Radford, (Ph. D. Dissertation), "The Reading and Speaking of Vachel Lindsay.", Northwestern University, (1951).
Pafford, Ruth Bishop, (M. A. Thesis), "Amy Lowell, Oral Interpreter.", University of Oklahoma, (1946).

Chapter IV

THE LITERATURE: CHOOSING MATERIALS FOR ORAL INTERPRETATION

Chloe Armstrong

The selection of worthy literary material is one of the chief concerns of the oral interpreter. This chapter discusses the development of a philosophy of choosing a selection and offers suggestions on locating materials appropriate to both the oral interpreter and the audience.

It is the oral interpreter who must discover what there is in a literary work that gives lasting value, what makes it worth reading. Many students do not feel qualified to evaluate the quality of a selection and turn to the literary critic for his opinion. Some students check the anthologists to see whether a certain story or poem has been considered worthy to be included. These approaches are good and should be encouraged, but at the same time the interpreter should be developing his own ability as a critic. He must gain confidence in his literary judgments.

The choosing of good literature or oral interpretation is a very personal judgment. Actually, the interpreter's selection of material involves his total range of experience, knowledge and appreciation. For in making a choice of a literary selection, the oral reader is offering something of himself. He is saying, "According to my understanding, this particular piece of literature is worthy of study and presentation." The more background we have, the more experience we have, the more opportunity for appreciation. The appreciation of any art implies discrimination and the ability to discriminate is one of the chief goals of education. The oral interpreter must learn in choosing his material to sort the valid from the phony, the good from the bad, and the great from the inferior. But the student is often faced with the dilemma of having to make a choice with a limited background of knowledge. He must select a piece of literature before he begins his preparation. In beginning courses, sometimes the instructor assigns most of the material, and therefore the problem is solved. But the good student must learn during his college career and the rest of his life to develop his own standard of evaluation. Margaret Robb says, "Other people may give valuable help but the actual experience in reading poems and developing standards by which to appraise them belongs to the individual reader."[1]

DEVELOPING A PHILOSOPHY
OF CHOOSING A SELECTION

The task of evaluating the quality of literature is a difficult one. Critical judgment is developed with study, experience, and time. Probably the most noteworthy and available source for the student in his study is the literary critic. Although the study of oral interpretation is not the study of literary criticism, the critic does provide special insights into literature which assist the reader in enhancing his own response. As Don Geiger points out, the oral interpreter may now think more seriously of the relationship of oral interpretation to literary study, and he may see in modern critical movement a recurring, ceaseless effort to approach even more closely the individual work of literary art.[2] And this approach to literary understanding can be very helpful to the oral interpreter not only in the selection of his material, but in the selection of quality literature.

However, the reader does not have to wait until he becomes a scholarly critic to have an opinion on the merit of literature and to choose a selection for oral interpretation. But he does have an obligation to himself and to his listener to avoid unworthy and appealing literature. Material of literary quality is all around, so the choice of poor literature is unfortunate and wholly unnecessary.

The question is often asked if it is permissible for the interpreter on some occasion to read inferior or even poor literature to a particular audience. Arguments offered by those who answer yes to the question may be divided into two general headings. First, a good reader can present the material in such an effective manner that it would be acceptable and enjoyable for the audience. And, second, that simple themes and ideas are often found in inferior literature.

It is true that a superior reader can interpret an inferior piece of literature and make it sound much better than it is, just as a fluent speaker can often make unworthy statements or half-truths sound truthful and lofty. Nevertheless, inferior literature remains inferior regardless of how it has been read, just as an untruth remains an untruth regardless of the lofty presentation. However, if the oral interpreter concludes that a presentation of a very light selection is appropriate for a particular audience, or certain occasion, he should offer it for what it is worth and not attempt to present it as great literature. Just as an opera singer in a special situation might step forward and sing a light popular number to the delight of the audience, the reader may give a poem, essay, or any selection of inferior quality. But he should indicate to his audience in his introduction or in the tone of his voice that he understands the frivolity of the material he is reading.

If the interpreter chooses material of literary quality, he offers a broader background of experience for himself and his listeners. Good literature has inherent qualities and intrinsic values which stimulate the interpreter and interest the audience. Oral interpretation can add new dimensions to material of literary merit. Actually the problem is one of selectivity and judgment. "Readers should use their time judiciously, surrounding themselves with literature which grows with repeated reading."[3]

In evaluating the second contention that simple themes and ideas which have a strong appeal to people are often found in poor and inferior literature, the student must not confuse profundity with complexity or popularity with inferiority. An experience may be profound even though the language with which the experience is expressed is simple. This kind of literary achievement has been illustrated by authors throughout the history of literature. John Donne, the Elizabethan poet, through the use of simple language, created the sonnet "Death, Be Not Proud" which has stood the test of time and maintained status over a period of years.[4] The same may be said of John Milton and his sonnet "On His Blindness." The poets of the twentieth century have relied on simple language, familiar images and scenes to create experiences such as W. H. Auden in his poem "Music des Beau Arts" or Dylan Thomas in "Fern Hill."

Two selections may have comparatively the same theme, supported by somewhat the same emotional value, and still, vary greatly in their status of literary quality. The difference may lie in the manner with which the author has used his elements of style to blend and mold the mood and theme. In a literary selection, the style adds or detracts from its status. In all literature there is behind each selection an intelligence—the author—who created in language the illusion of the experience; thus it is not a direct experience, but one man's account that is created in terms that are conditioned by the *form* in which he is writing. When the selection is said to have a simple, life-like theme, the reader should compare it to another of the same theme and examine the creation as conditioned by the form and style in which it was written.[5] A simple shallow theme, lightly and poorly treated should be avoided. The accomplishment of selecting and preparing a worthy piece of literature is much more rewarding.

As the student learns more about the form of literature and the process that produces the form, he will develop his skill in discrimination and judgment. But it takes time and much more experience.

LOCATING A LITERARY SELECTION

After the student has formed a philosophy as basis for his choice of a literary selection, he must answer further and more specific questions as they apply to his philosophical concept. On what basis shall he make the choice or where shall he begin? Although there are no set rules, the following suggestions may be helpful. First, begin where you are: what writers and selections do you know? Consider the different authors that have been introduced in your English classes. T. S. Elliot is a familiar name to most English and interpretative reading students. If the student's reading of Elliot is limited to the poem "The Hollow Men," he can broaden his acquaintance to include other poems such as "Burnt Norton," "Four Quartets," "Portrait of a Lady," "Love Song of Prufrock," "Ash Wednesday," "The Wasteland." Read extensively Elliot's writing and discover his less familiar poems and his essays, stories and poetic dramas.

Such procedure should be followed for other poets with which the student has some acquaintance. Too often students limit reading to two or three of the most popular poems of a poet and never know a large scope of the author's writing. Many poets, such as T. S. Elliot, Dylan Thomas, and W. H. Auden, also have written essays, stories, and dramas. Begin where you are. The student should not hesitate to acknowledge his limitation in literature. But he should further his knowledge through extensive reading.

Although poetry is often the most popular form of interpretive literature, the reader should include other forms, such as essay, short story, novel, drama, letters and biographies. The literary letters and the biographies, although often overlooked, offer new material for the oral interpreter. "The letter appears to be the highest quality of literature for the oral interpreter," states Louis Kronenberger.[6] In discussing the value of the biography for the oral interpreter, Alan Jones points out, "In a century in which the emphasis is placed upon reality, critics and oral readers have found that reality of the lives and experiences of real people adds a certain amount of glamor to the necessary touch of truth."[7]

The same procedure should be followed in broadening the reader's knowledge of each type of literature. Take an inventory of your reading knowledge of each of the above types of literature. If you discover you are familiar with one or two selections, essay, story, or drama, of an author, explore several unfamiliar selections by the same author.

These suggestions can serve as the first step in developing a broad reading background, but it is not enough. An oral interpreter will want to select literature that will open new vistas and make new discoveries. This second step can be accomplished by reading widely and wisely. Some students have limited their reading to one period of writing: They cherish the classics and loath the contemporary, or they frown on classics and praise the modern. Other students proclaim a love for English literature but avoid American authors. No one age of literature or nation has a monopoly on producing good literature. If the student has developed a strong affinity for one particular age of literature or to the literary works of one nation, let him turn to another age or another country and make new discoveries. His new discoveries will not only broaden his background but may deepen his appreciation for his first choice, for as Don Geiger says, "Of course we believe that the literary person, writer or reader, though he may be in his fulfillment merely a prodigal son come to some home or another, nevertheless knows better what kind of home it is than all those sons and daughters who have never been away."8

A third suggestion, which underlies the other two suggestions and serves as motivation for any choice of material, is the interest of the oral reader. The student should begin by asking himself what claims his attention most? Students vary in their interests and activities. Some like to explore and travel to new places, see new sights, while others prefer history and tradition. Therefore, consider yourself and what *you* like. This does not mean that the interpreter should never read what he does not like, for we often dislike what we do not understand. But it does suggest that the student's special likes should lead him to other likes, other interests and other discoveries. It is through new discoveries, different interests, and new perspectives that the reader developes his taste and judgment.

The question is often asked if the reader must agree or sympathize with the ideas or experience expressed in the material he is reading. It is true that the oral interpreter must understand his material and have a keen interest in the literary selection he has chosen to read, but this does not imply that the reader must accept or reject statements in literature as observations on life and philosophy. Rather, the interpreter should recognize and understand the statement as it is related to the function and purpose of literature. Wallace Bacon, in answering this question, points out, "We can believe in literary worlds which we would not accept at all as real worlds."9 It is this reason that makes literature exciting and wonderful. You will find further comments on this point in the next chapter.

KNOWING THE AUDIENCE
AND THE OCCASION

The type of material presented is largely the decision of the reader, but the student should be careful to choose selections that will be suitable for the audience and occasion. The scholar in the field of public address has long been aware of the importance of the audience and speaking situation. The oral interpreter should consider his listeners as carefully as the public speaker. The psychology of the audience is of particular interest to the reader. It is true that students of oral interpretation will be choosing literary selections primarily for class assignments, but all oral interpreters, whether they read in special reading hours, in the classroom, or to a social, religious, or civic club, must be sensitive to the audience and occasion. For the purpose of oral interpretation and its final objective is the experiencing of the literature by the audience.

The reader should make an analysis of the audience and situation. By making inquiries of those responsible for arranging the program, he can gain much information as to the educational level, and cultural background of a audience. For it is obvious that one does not usually read the same material to a teenage group that he would read to a retired teachers' group, nor to a womens' church group that he would read to a Chamber of Commerce. The size of the audience may be large or small, but the oral interpreter should think of them as people. Usually individual members of an audience are influenced by the character of the group, and therefore the group reacts as a single person during a performance. With this information in mind, the reader can more easily prick and enlarge the sensibilities of the listeners in order that they may react to the material being read.

The occasion for the reading is another factor to be considered. Why have the people gathered? If the occasion is primarily to hear this particular person, the reader has more freedom in his choice of material. But if the reading is only a part, sometimes a small part, of the total program, the reader must choose selections that will be appropriate with the total program and harmonize with the mood and attitude of the listeners. There are several factors that may influence the mood and reaction of the audience, such as time of day, the kind of weather, the place of gathering. Temperaments of people differ at different times of the day; therefore, the reader must be sure that his selection or selections fit the hour of the occasion. A reader who presents a tragedy such as "Hamlet" or "King Lear" to an audience in the morning or at a luncheon program will not usually receive a sympathetic response. However, the same audience, when it has been properly prepared, might respond to the material at eight o'clock in the evening.

The audience usually has a courteous and friendly attitude toward the reader. Seldom does the interpreter encounter a hostile feeling from his listeners. They want to enjoy the program.

The reader should have the same courtesy for his listeners by recognizing the significance of the occasion, the friendliness of the people, and by observing the time alloted to him. If the reader is sharing the program, he should consider what will precede and what will follow and how much time has been allotted each person. Readers should be particularly careful to stay within their time limits.

When the student understands the audience and occasion, he is faced with a practical and important question: Where do I find good literature to share with the listener? The answer is not so difficult; all the reader needs to do is to look for it. Consult your English and oral interpretation textbooks.[10] Check the bibliographies of books for further suggestions of sources. There are many anthologies and special collections available in the library. Book lists of recommended reading are often found posted in classrooms and libraries. Well-prepared indexes are available to the student to help him locate the material he wants. The student can gain a wider acquaintance with all types of literature by browsing through the library. There are many good anthologies of works of one author or collections of the different forms of literature now available in paperback editions. Material suitable for oral interpretation is all around us; it only requires some one to look for it. The sincere discerning person will find it.

SUMMARY

The selection of the right material is of major concern to any artist. The theatre director often must spend much time in finding the right play, one that is suitable for his actors and his audience. The oral interpreter is no exception; he too is faced with the question of: "What shall I read?" There are no easy answers, and no one can formulate a set of hard and fast rules. But there are several factors the oral reader must consider. He should consider the literary quality of the material, the nature of the occasion, the special interest of the audience and his own capabilities. The interpreter's final decision should be based on a studied judgment of all the factors involved. The reader who explores literature will continue the search and this search will lead him to the library and all available sources for suitable reading material.

FOOTNOTES

[1]Mary Margaret Robb, "Growing A Taste for Poetry," *The Speech Teacher,* Vol. 12, No. 4 (November, 1963, pp. 317-322.

[2]Don Geiger, *The Sound, Sense, and Performance of Literature* (Chicago, Illinois: Scott, Forseman and Company, 1963), p. 7.

[3]Armstrong and Brandes, *The Oral Interpretation of Literature* (New York: McGraw-Hill Book Company, Inc., 1963, p. 45.

[4]*Ibid.,* p. 32.

[5]Additional suggestions and illustrations in the study of developing literary judgment are available in other textbooks of oral interpretation: Aggertt and Bowen, *Communicative Reading,* second edition (New York: Macmillan Company, 1963), pp.24-28; Armstrong and Brandes, *The Oral Communication of Literature.* (New York: McGraw-Hill Book Company, Inc., 1963), pp. 37-54.

[6]Louis Kronenberger, "The Art of Letter Writing," *Atlantic Monthly* (March, 1966), p. 99.

[7]Alan P. Jones, "The Reality of Real People," *Commonwealth* (October 22, 1965), pp. 88-93.

[8]Don Geiger, *op. cit.,* p. 21.

[9]Wallace A. Bacon, *The Art of Interpretation* (New York: Holt, Rinehart and Winston, 1966), p. 124.

[10]For suggested bibliographies of materials suitable for oral interpretation, see: Aggert and Bowen, *Communicative Reading,* second edition (New York: Macmillan Company, 1963), pp. 30-38. Armstrong, *ibid.,* pp. 56-60. Bacon and Breen, *Literature as Experience* (New York: McGraw-Hill Book Company, Inc., 1959).

FURTHER READINGS

BOOKS

Aggertt, Otis J. and Elbert Bowen, *Communicative Reading.* The Macmillan Company, New York, 1964.

Armstrong, Chloe and Paul Brandes, *The Oral Interpretation of Literature.* McGraw-Hill Book Company, Inc., New York, 1963.

Bacon, Wallace A., *The Art of Interpretation.* Holt, Rinehart, and Winston, Inc., New York, 1966.

Burke, Kenneth. *The Philosophy of Literary Form.* Vintage Books, 1957.

Geeting, Baxter M., *Interpretation for Our Time.* W. M. Brown Company, Dubuque, Iowa, 1966.

Geiger, Don, *The Sound, Sense, and Performance of Literature.* Scott, Forseman and Company, Chicago, Illinois, 1963.

Wellek, Rene and Austin Warren, *Theory of Literature.* Harcourt, Brace and World, Inc., New York, 1956.

Chapter V

THE ANALYSIS: A NOTE ON VALUE ORIENTATIONS

J. A. Hendrix and John W. Gray

This chapter on analysis is unique in that it focuses on one neglected area in literary analysis: that of recognizing the writer's value system and using this knowledge to improve the accuracy of the interpretation.

After the interpreter has made his choice of literary material his next step is analysis. It is not difficult to find many excellent discussions of literary analysis specifically designed for the oral interpreter. They vary from the one chapter versions in basic oral interpretation textbooks[1] to the elaborate full texts devoted solely to the subject.[2] There is hardly a text in the entire oral interpretation area which does not emphasize the need for gaining a complete understanding of the literary work as a first step in preparing for oral performance. This close scrutiny is essential for total understanding, and knowledge of the many subtle details of plot, character, and structure will result in improved oral performance.

One area of analysis often neglected by the oral interpreter is that of *value orientations.* There is a certain subtlety required on the part of the oral interpreter in determining the author's value system and in using this knowledge in improving his interpretation. It is the purpose of this chapter to provide a few guidelines useful in analyzing these value systems found in literary works.

VALUE ORIENTATIONS IN DRAMATIC AND NARRATIVE MATERIAL

The oral interpreter's analysis of narrative or dramatic literature usually includes an examination of such elements of this material as setting, theme, point of view, plot, characterization, and dialogue as a prelude to oral presentation. Among the most basic delineations which the interpreter must make are, of course, identification of the protagonist and antagonist, and the nature of the conflict between these two entities (man against man, man against nature, or man against himself). The protagonist traditionally has been defined as the hero or heroine of the work: the representative of the forces which may be characterized as morally "good". The antagonist, the force or persons pitted against the protagonist, traditionally has been associated, in some degree, with that which may be characterized as morally "evil". Hence the conflict has actually been defined in terms of an underlying *value system.*

In more traditional works of literature, the author's value system has most often conformed to that of his readers and to the societal group within which he wrote. In his prescriptive observations, Aristotle, for example, seems to have assumed the existence of a concept of moral goodness which was commonly held between the poet or dramatist and his audience:

> In the Characters there are four points to aim at. First and foremost, that they shall be good. There will be an element of character in the play, if (as has been observed) what a personage says or does reveals a certain moral purpose; and a good element of character, if the purpose so revealed is good.[3]

Aristotle seems to have recognized the existence of certain societal values which governed the behavior of men to the extent that these values should be reflected in man's literary representations of himself.[4] The Greeks, of course, were not content, as were their descendants, with subtle characterizations. They dressed their protagonists and antagonists in identifying masks, so that value association would be unmistakable. Although blatant, theirs was a literary conception of man as a being endowed with reason, will, and a sense of values; and it survived largely intact in Western literature until the twentieth century. The hero-protagonist, then was an obvious and inevitable literary product of a humanistic tradition in society.

It would be superfluous to chronicle here the general de-humanization of society and the accompanying rise of such philosophies as determinism and relativism in the twentieth century.[5] Joseph Wood Krutch has perceptively expressed the nature of the ensuing conflict between the surviving humanistic-moralistic spirit of Greek conception and the valuelessness of our technologically oriented twentieth century society:

> The universe revealed by science, especially the sciences of biology and psychology, is one in which the human spirit cannot find a comfortable home. That spirit breathes freely only in a universe where what philosophers call Value Judgments are of supreme importance. It needs to believe, for instance, that right and wrong are real, that Love is more than a biological function, that the human mind is capable of reason rather than merely of rationalization, and that it has the power to will and to choose instead of being compelled merely to react in the fashion predetermined by its conditioning. Since science has proved that none of these beliefs is more than a delusion, mankind will be compelled either to surrender what we call its humanity by adjusting to the real world or to live some kind of tragic existence in a universe alien to the deepest needs of its nature.[6]

This head-on collision between the old values and the new technology, perhaps as well as any source, accounts for the recurrent themes of valuelessness, amorality, and allienation in contemporary literature. Whatever the cause of these themes, their presence is undeniable. As one respected faculty colleague aptly describes the practitioners of his art, "the contemporary dramatist often treats man as though he were an insect. Without moralizing, he simply sticks a pin into man and watches him wiggle."[7]

We must be careful, however, not to condemn a literary work merely because of our reaction to its subject matter. In his discussion of the problem of presenting evil in art, William Grace makes this point well when he says:

> The presentation of evil does not in itself constitute immorality. Always to be kept in mind is the distinction between the evil which the artist imitates and the viewpoint . . . he brings to bear upon the evil he represents. It does not follow that a mimesis of sin and evil in a work of art implies that an artist approves of them or that he intends the reader to approve of them. Immorality in a work of art becomes evident only when an artist 'glorifies' evil and suggests it as a suitable pattern for human conduct.8

It might be noted at this point that a central determinant of morality itself is the prevailing value structure of a given societal unit. Self-righteous moralists among us may denounce the depravity of a particular author, as Grace suggests, simply because he may glorify "evil" or recommend a pattern of behavior which happens not to reflect their own system of values. By definition, moral judgments must be made according to accepted societal codes of behavior. It remains for the individual interpreter, however, to determine whether a moral evaluation of a work of literature is really relevant to the artistic worth of the literature; or whether the work, because it may be "immoral", is any less valid as a genuine reflection of human experience. A great writer may create a synthesis or fusion of many legimate approaches to truth as he sees it. Even that which may be regarded as a perverted sense of values can be expressed with great skill, and it is usually these literary pieces that create confusion in the mind of the reader as he catalogues the "masterpieces" and the "trash". Jacques Maritain explained the predicament in this manner:

> The essential question is not to know if a novelist can or cannot paint a particular aspect of evil. The essential question is to know at what height he places himself to make this painting, and if his heart and his art is pure enough, and strong enough, to make it without connivance.9

One fact that seems clearly to emerge is that no author can avoid making a value statement. If the oral interpreter accepts this premise, then in order to fully understand his material, he must also accept the responsibility of discovering what the author's value statement is.

Milton states that his aim in *Paradise Lost* is to "justify" the ways of God to men". Many themes other than this, however, are suggested in a complex work of this nature. It is also possible for a writer to deliberately set out to do one thing, but to accomplish another. Should, then the writer's intent be relaxed in order to reveal more, possibly, than he intended? Northrop Frye declares that it "takes a great deal of will power to write poetry, but part of that will power must be employed in trying to relax the will, so making a large part of one's writing involuntary."[10] The task, therefore, of discovering the value statement is not always easy, especially in the study of contemporary literature which may express what Saul Bellow's Moses Herzog calls "the Wasteland outlook".

At this point we would like to suggest to the oral interpreter a specific procedure for analyzing the value statement inherent in narrative or dramatic material. Interpreters are generally instructed in their analysis to seek in all areas the author's intent. In this analysis we recommend a thorough investigation of the *value orientations* of the main characters involved and of their societal unit.

AUTHOR'S LITERARY METHOD

A first consideration in determining value structures in assessment of the author's literary method. As Wellek and Warren advise on this point:

> ...much the most common approach to the relations of literature and society is the study of the works of literature and social documents, as assumed pictures of social reality. Nor can it be doubted that some kind of social picture can be abstracted from literature.
>
> But such studies seem of little value so long as they take it for granted that literature is simply a mirror of life, a reproduction, and thus, obviously, a social document. Such studies make sense only if we know the artistic method of the novelist studied, can say—not merely in general terms, but concretely—in what relation the picture stands to the social reality. Is it realistic by intention? Or is it, at certain points, satire, caricature, or romantic idealization?"[11]

We must discover how the author's artistic purpose is served by technique. Is the author making a direct, straightforward approach in presenting his picture, or is he interposing between the reader and the picture the hints, exaggerations, and insinuations which color and reveal his point of view? Designation of artistic method, then, will be a key preliminary factor in assessing the author's expression of values.

THE SOCIETAL VALUE SYSTEM

Having discovered the author's artistic method, the interpreter should, secondly, examine the overall value structure of the societal unit within which the characters operate. At this point, he may wish to enlist the aid of scholars who have studied the value system of the societal group or unit which serves as a setting for his literary selection. If, for instance, he has chosen to interpret American literature, the findings of Steele and Redding[12] may provide a useful framework of social values. Their general outline of American values includes "Puritan and Pioneer Morality", "The Value of the Individual", "Achievement and Success", "Change and Progress", "Ethical Equality", "Equality of Opportunity", "Effort and Optimism", "Efficiency, Practicality, and Pragmatism", "Rejection of Authority", "Science and Secular Rationality", "Sociality", "Material Comfort", "Quantification", "External Conformity", "Humor", "Generosity and 'Considerateness' ", and "Patriotism". There are obvious variations in this value system corresponding to particular locales or ethnic groups within the United States. The interpreter, of course, needs to account for these variations. But his initial task in discovering the value statement of the literary work is that of creating an overall value typology for a discrete societal unit.

VALUES AND MAJOR CHARACTERS

The interpreter's third task in assessing the author's value statement is the association of values with the major characters involved in the work. The characters' value orientations—expressed positively or negatively—are reflected in the action, dialogue, and other aspects of the work in which characterization is developed. In the analysis of traditional literature, it should be possible to identify protagonists and antagonists according to their correspondence, or lack of it, to the value system of their society. It may become apparent to the oral interpreter, however, that the author being studied has created a new set of values and that the protagonist-antagonist should be re-defined in terms of the author's set of values rather than the values held by his society. In any event, the value orientations of the main characters will provide the oral interpreter with an indispensable key to their conditioning and behavior.

CHARACTER VALUES
AND SOCIETAL VALUES

Finally, the interpreter should draw comparisons between character values and societal values as they appear in his material. But he should carefully avoid mixing "worlds", or superimposing a character from one society upon the value structure of another society. One European anti-hero for instance, is introduced with caution to American readers: "That a man so young, so contemptuous of 'seriousness', frankly absorbed in his own ego to the point of pathology from an American middle-class psychiatric position, should break through every predictable human prejudice by the sheer authenticity of his being is a significant event that separates this book from 'literature' at the same time that it inevitably creates its own place in literature which has no precise equal for it."[13] The character's degree of identification with or alienation from the values of his own societal unit, however, may well provide the interpreter with insight into what the author deems valuable in life. And this statement of value is the objective of the oral interpreter's axiological analysis of his material.

CONCLUSION

As a part of the preliminary analysis of his material the oral interpreter may wish to include a study of the value orientations incorporated within the work. This aspect of his analysis includes four steps. First, he should examine the author's artistic method to determine the degree of literal reality represented in the work. Second, the interpreter should devise an overall value system for the societal unit which serves as the setting. Third, he should assess the value orientations of the major characters involved. Finally, by comparing and contrasting the value orientations of the characters and those of the societal setting, he may discover the overall value statement inherent in the work. Having discovered the author's value statement, the oral interpreter may use it either as an aid to understanding his material or as a platform from which to proclaim the author's "morality" or the lack of it. Perhaps the value statement is most meaningful when placed in the perspective suggested by David Daiches; "Our only axiom is that man, as a 'doing and suffering' creature, is interesting, is worth contemplating and trying to understand, and that his experience is significant to us because it is his experience and for no other reason."[14]

FOOTNOTES

[1]For a good example see Jere Veilleux, *Oral Interpretation: The Recreation of Literature* (New York, 1967), Chapter 2.

[2]See Thomas Sloan, *The Oral Study of Literature* (New York, 1966).

[3]*"Poetics," Introduction to Aristotle.* Trans. Richard McKeon (New York, 1947), p. 643.

[4]The association of rhetorical theory and discourse with a system of moral values is also evident in the works of Plato, Aristotle, Isocrates, Cicero, and Quintilian. This suggests a general union of discourse—both rhetorical and poetic—with moral values. For a discussion of the relationship of axiology to rhetoric, see Ralph T. Eubanks and Virgil L. Baker, "Toward an Axiology of Rhetoric", *Quarterly Journal of Speech,* XLVIII (April, 1962), pp. 157-168.

[5]For an interesting and highly readable account of this phenomenon in American culture, see Henry May, *The End of American Innocence* (New York, 1959).

[6]*The Modern Temper* (New York, 1956), p. xi.

[7]From a conversation with Professor F. Cowles Strickland of the Department of Speech Arts at the American University.

[8]William Grace, *Response to Literature* (New York, 1965), p. 26.

[9]Jacques Maritain, *Art and Scholasticism* (New York, 1949), p.171.

[10]Northrop Frye, *Anatomy of Criticism: Four Essays* (Princeton, New Jersey, 1957), p. 88.

[11]Rene Wellek and Austin Warren, *Theory of Literature* (New York, 1956), pp. 91-92.

[12]Edward D. Steele and W. Charles Redding, "The American Value System: Premises for Persuasion", *Western Speech,* XXVI (Spring, 1962), pp. 83-91.

[13]Seymour Krim, "Introduction," *I Jan Cremer. An Autobiographical Novel* (New York, 1965), p. vii.

[14]David Daiches, *A Study of Literature: For Readers and Critics* (Ithaca, 1948), p. 229.

FURTHER READINGS

BOOKS

Beebe, Maurice, *Literary Symbolism: An Introduction to the Interpretation of Literature.* Wadsworth Publishing Company, San Francisco, 1960.

Daiches, David, *Critical Approaches to Literature.* Prentice-Hall, Inc., Englewood Cliffs, New Jersey, 1956.

Gogel, Nikolai, *Dead Souls.* Trans. Bernard Guilbert Guerney, Holt, Rinehart and Winston, New York, 1961.

Huxley, Aldous, *Vulgarity in Literature.* Harper and Rowe, New York, 1940.

Lowes, John Livingston, *Convention and Revolt in Poetry.* Houghton-Mifflin Company, Boston, 1919.

Maritain, Jacques, *Art and Faith.* Trans. E. de P. Maltheus, Philosophical Library Inc., New York, 1943.

Quiller-Couch, Sir Arthur, *The Poet as Citizen and Other Papers.* Cambridge University Press, New York, 1935.

Scott, Wilbur, *Five Approaches of Literary Criticism.* The Macmillan Company, New York, 1962.

Tolstoi, Leo, *What Is Art?* Trans. Alymer Mande, Oxford University Press, Fair Lawn, New Jersey, 1959.

Chapter VI

THE RESPONSE: A DISCUSSION OF EMPATHY

Joyce F. Horton

Empathic response is another major concern of the oral interpreter. This chapter discusses the nature of empathy, presents a few selected theories, and relates them to the oral interpreter's art.

Much consideration has been given to the term "empathy," its origin and use, by writers in the fields of philosophy, psychology, aesthetics and communication. By its most common definition empathy is a wordless interactional process between two people or more or between an individual and an inanimate object; it implies the transmission of knowledge and feeling. A study of this phenomenon is particularly relevant to aesthetic experience and the field of oral interpretation because empathy presumably engenders aesthetic response and is an aid in interactional situations. Therefore, the purpose of this chapter is to gain a better understanding of the nature and theories of empathy. In this sense the problems posed by literary re-creation and appreciation - the oral interpreter's tasks - may be partially solved.

The oral interpreter's function is that of re-embodying a literary work. In this act he is especially responsible for expressing fully the intended aesthetic experience. The result is one of shared experience among the interpreter, the work expressed, and the listener. The term "empathy" describes the oral interpreter's discovery of, and response to, the emotional complex and meaning inherent in the literary object. In contrast, "empathic process" refers to the steps leading to this discovery. The phenomenon of empathy implies then a transmission of the logical and emotional content. Ultimately its use may enable the reader to find a selection's intended meaning, and to experience aesthetically the work as well. The use of empathy may also enlarge the listener's understanding, appreciation, and capacity to respond. Therefore, in oral interpretation empathy is a process in which words come alive, take on meaning, and enrich the literary act.

Although there is considerable agreement regarding empathy's general meaning, theoreticians and experimenters alike have failed to specify an exact definition. To some it is an innately divine art, a sixth sense, which entails a listening with the third ear. To others it is simply an acquired technique based on systematic effort and conscious endeavor. Additional confusion is evidenced by a review of the journals and oral interpretation textbooks. Opinions vary regarding the specific procedure involved in the empathic process. For the most part the writers have not "isolated" empathy, but have correlated it with related processes such as Identification, Insight, Projection, Role-Playing and Sympathy.[1] The interchangeable use of these terms with empathy not only is misleading, but also implies that each related process may be employed in its own right to enhance the empathic effect. This may or may not be the case.[2] Therefore, oral interpreters need to identify empathy separately from these similar processes.

The origin of empathy may best be traced in terms of its basic premise, that each individual functions both as a communicant and a communicator of information. It is along these lines that David Stewart, a psychoanalyst interested in counselor-counselee relations, traces the development of empathy. Stewart, in his book, *Preface to Empathy,* asserts that the concept is over 2,000 years old and is one alluded to by Plato, Aristotle, St. John, Plotinus, St. Augustine, Aquinas, Spinoza, and Kant. In their writings, according to Stewart, the basic thesis is that personal knowing is the key, not only to self-knowledge, knowledge of other people, and knowledge of the outer world, but also to all knowledge as well. In this respect the writings are considered intrinsic reflections of the concept of empathy.[3]

Another author, Robert L. Katz, in *Empathy, Its Nature and Uses,* offers a second theory of empathy's origin. The "Once We Were One" theory maintains that humanity is simply the evolution of an original common source. This hypothesis asserts that mankind was initially integrated into a larger whole, achieving individual existence as a product later. Accordingly, every individual carries traces of the native genetic unity; the empathic process, the understanding of others, is possible because it is simply an act of "re-cognition," a re-awakening to what was once common property. Therefore, the perception of another being is possible because "once we were one" and because we are born to understand and to comprehend others. Because of its past, the individual ego remains common and undifferentiated. When it apprehends the feelings of others in empathy, it once more experiences the sense of being part of a larger whole.[4] Katz refers to the writings of Freud as verification of the theory: "The ego feeling we are aware of now is thus only a shrunken vestige of a far more extensive feeling - a feeling which embraced the universe and expressed an inseparable connection of the ego with the external world."[5] Stewart and Katz reflect two of the many theories which have been suggested on the origin of empathy.

Throughout empathy's development the theorists used such labels as "insight," "illumination," and "mysticism," in their description of the phenomenon. One writer, Theodor Lipps, originated a different term. In 1897, Lipps, a German psychoanalyst, published an account of human behavior in relation to aesthetic appreciation and employed the term "einfühlung" as a description of the individual's response to the art object. Edward D. Titchener, a Cornell psychology professor, later coined the term "empathy" as an English equivalent of the original "einfühlung." Titchener is also credited with the modern usage in this country. The fundamental idea of empathy, however, is one which has long been attended to by various writers and theoreticians.

Research findings indicate that the concept of empathy is receiving wide application. Undoubtedly this is due to two factors: (1) the impression that empathy results in self-understanding, the understanding of others, and an understanding of the outer world, and (2) the general acknowledgement that empathic responses underlie each communicative act. Application of empathy is made by those in psychology, philosophy, the aesthetic areas, and in fact, by all who are interested in the communication process itself.

In the aesthetic areas of creation and appreciation there is much recognition of the importance and use of empathy. Ethelyn Pearson comments on empathy's literary merit by calling it an extra-sensory quality that adds depth to a story. Creatively, she adds that "a story without empathy leaves its readers devoid of feeling, always on the surface, never once does he get into the writer's confidence."[6] A specific example of the phenomenon's utilitarian value is evidenced in the writings of G. K. Chesterton. Chesterton's famous character, Father Brown, consistently solved mysteries by empathizing with the criminal. In relation to aesthetic appreciation, Irving Lorge's study of communicator-communicatee effectiveness finds that a lack of empathy results in poor comprehension of written or oral materials. He refers to this as "...lack of community between the expresser and understander."[7] H. A. Overstreet, who has also written on empathy in relation to communication, implies the enormous future possibilities:

> Empathy is one of our human potentials and it can go far toward saving man from psychic isolation.[8]

Those who have an aesthetic and behavioral interest, as well as those interested in the communication process itself, continue to debate the origin, meaning and use of empathy. Admittedly the phenomenon has received much historical attention. Presumably it elevates mere words and scattered thoughts to more meaningful realms, even though the exact procedure by which this is accomplished remains undetermined. Because empathy is considered an influential directive in interaction and vital to the process of communication, it will continue to command the research spotlight.

PSYCHOLOGICAL RESEARCH ON EMPATHIC ABILITY AND RELATED PERSONALITY CHARACTERISTICS

Psychologists acknowledge that empathic ability is related to the individual's ability to be empathized with. Stewart considers the phenomenon grounded in good-will and requiring personal effort. It is his opinion that the good-will individual is not only receptive to other individuals, but kindly disposes toward them as well. Consequently, when confronted with the interactional situation he appropriately makes some conscious attempt or movement toward communication.[9] In this respect it may be said that empathy and good-will are directly related, for empathy requires the attitude of constant readiness to respond to situations and objects. Psychologists also confirm that the individual's communication threshhold is dependent upon his approach-avoidance orientation. Personal effort comprises a strong motivation to comprehend and understand the feelings of others. Admittedly this requires energy, a factor attested to by Gregory Zilboorg, who once wrote of the involvement required in understanding historical figures:

> One must mobilize, not anesthetize one's feelings, revitalize all strivings, and even weaknesses and passions; otherwise it will be totally impossible to put one's self in the place of Alexander the Great, or Jesse James or Cromwell or Julius Caesar or the humblest slave of ancient Rome.[10]

Because the complete personality is reawakened in the empathic process, the empathizing individual must trust his emotions. One calculated risk is that latent stirrings and inadequately repressed feelings may surface consciously as part of the process. In this sense empathy is akin to Pandora's box, for the individual does not really know what he will discover. It is hardly surprising that many individuals thereby avoid altogether such emotional stimulation. Instead of fearlessly offering themselves to the empathic experience, they prevent if from happening by establishing certain barriers and prohibiting controls. Empathy, however, requires a demonstration of "good-faith," or a willingness to be exposed, and demands that the individual give himself to the experience.

Besides the requirement of getting involved, empathic ability also depends on a flexible ego. It is said that when such an ego is at its height, it is "...an ego formation in which the ego boundaries can change rapidly and easily but remain stable at any time if a standpoint must be held or defended."[11] Such an ego is skillfully able to move from one feeling state, or "state of mind," to another and is able to proceed without being confronted with conflict or hardship. The bard which William Hazlett describes possesses just such an ego, and was

> ...nothing in himself, but he was all that others were, or that they could become. He not only had in himself the germs of every faculty and feeling, but he could follow them by anticipation, intuitively into all their conceivable ramifications, through every change of thought.... He had only to think of anything in order to become that thing, with all the circimstances belonging to it.[12]

The psychological research on empathic ability and related personality characteristics bears important implications for the oral interpreter. He should realize that empathic ability relates to: (1) an ability to be empathized with, (2) depends on personal effort and good-will, (3) demands energy and self-trust, and (4) comprises a flexible ego. More importantly, he should fully attempt to utilize these guidelines in the oral interpretation experience.

THEORIES OF EMPATHY

It is generally agreed that empathy is a knowledge which cannot be verbalized. Significant thinkers have not looked upon the empathic response as a fixity - as an Absolute or a Universal - because the relation between what is done and what is undergone varies from individual to individual. In this respect, various theories of empathy have emerged. Of the four major theories - The Lipps Theory of Empathy, The Kinesthetic Theory of Empathy, The Gestalt Theory of Empathy, and The Play Theory of Empathy - only the first two will be discussed in this chapter because of their particular relevance to aesthetic experience, art theory, and oral interpretation.[13]

A. The Lipps Theory of Empathy

Theodor Lipps is credited with formulating the most systematic account of empathy in existence. His doctrine is that the object of art acquires meaning only because the individual projects his own ego or imagination into it. Hence the concept of "einfühlung" denotes a "feeling into," and asserts the dynamic quality of perception.

Lipps initially used an example of the appreciation of architecture to illustrate his meaning. He said that when an individual views an object, he experiences an understanding of the forces and tensions involved only by drawing analogies between these and his own personal experiences. In the same fashion he then experiences muscle and joint sensations similar to those he would have known had he actually constructed the object. It is the ideas of these sensations, which are projected into the object, which give the object life and meaning. By the same token, these projected sensations become attributes of the object and thus, no longer reside in the individual. In respect to this activity, Lipps states that perception alone cannot be regarded as the answer. In explanation he states that the conception of an object's inherent movement is possible only when the individual has the equivalent knowledge of the process of construction. This is to say that the empathic process is based on the idea of an *a priori* similarity and that the individual's inner activity is a reservoir of feelings which consequently may be catalyzed and set into motion by the sight of a specific object.

This view on the dynamic element of perception is the essence of Lipps' theory of empathy. Although in his early writings Lipps included physiological or kinesthetic factors, he later emphasized the metaphysical or ego-projection approach to empathy. This subsequent psychological basis which Lipps gave empathy is called the science of the mind, and involves the "individual consciousness." The latter refers not to consciousness in general, but to a real, rather than imagined, state of the self or mind. Lipps specifies that feelings are conscious activities which accompany perception and further categorizes his treatment of empathy as follows:

1. Empathy is self-objectivation; "the objectivation of myself in an object distinguished from myself."
2. Aesthetic empathy incorporates the general form of empathy, but is also a special and unique form of empathy.[14]

In relation to the first category, self-objectivation, it may be said that all feelings are self-feeling. Since the theorist believed that the individual feels himself into the object and experiences the feelings he would have in that position, Lipps noted the results of empathizing with various objects. Accordingly, his findings assert that if the object's movements are smooth, generous, and balanced, as in the case of a graceful curve, pleasantness results; if the movements instead are jerky, confined, and strained, as illustrated in the leaning tower of Pisa, unpleasantness occurs.[15] The resulting effect of self-objectivation is perhaps best described by Robert Vischer: "It [the individual] recognizes its second self, how it sits - changed - in the object, and takes it back into itself."[16] Lipps' viewpoint may thus be taken to mean that the feelings which are said to be attributes of the object are in actuality those which have been designated as such by the individual. Or phrased another way, in self-objectivation the individual attributes feelings and emotions to inanimate objects.

In respect to aesthetic theory the ideas of Lipps fall under the following headings:

1. The Aesthetic Object
2. Aesthetic Contemplation
3. The Aesthetic Experience

Lipps defines the nature of the aesthetic object as consisting of the "sensous appearance," nor the tangible, physical object, but the impressions as modified by the imagination and so charged with vital significance. The attribution of life and character flows into the expressiveness of the object only when the object signifies life and character. In judging a thing beautiful, Lipps thus warns the individual not to transfer beauty to the object, but rather to use expressions like "I see this form as symmetrical." In view of his writings there can be little doubt that the theorist appreciated the importance of the aesthetic object as a *stimulus* of the aesthetic experience.

In examining the second aspect of Lipps' aesthetic theory, aesthetic contemplation, we find that the theory incorporates sensations of striving and tensions. The aim of such activity is a well-integrated attitude. Thus in aesthetic contemplation the individual feels himself advancing toward a goal, resisting and overcoming obstacles, and in effect, experiencing a multifarious activity. Lipps clearly specifies, however, that such striving is <u>not</u> the result of a literal enactment, i.e., the actual innervation of muscles. Instead it is the result of the individual's "motor imagination." Although the possibility of spontaneous mimicry is recognized (in contemplating statue, for example, the individual may involuntarily imitate its posture and apparent movement by readjusting his own muscles and physique), Lipps nevertheless insists that empathy is not composed of feelings so aroused. This is to say that even though contemplation of the object's observed movement catalyzes the desire to an equivalent self-activity, such activity need not be kinesthetic, but merely mental. Lipps admittedly recognizes that feelings are conscious activities. He specifies, however, that the individual becomes correspondingly less aware of the inner activity as he becomes more involved in the act of contemplation. In effect, the movements which the observer feels are applied to the object, and his attention is directed toward the object and absorbed therein. The result is that the individual is entirely and wholly identical with the object of contemplation.[17]

In relation to the aesthetic experience, Lipps acknowledges that the aesthetic feelings involve two special forms: aesthetic enjoyment and aesthetic pleasure. He comments on the former as follows:

> The question about the object of aesthetic enjoyment may be answered in a two-fold manner; on the one hand, it can be said that esthetic pleasure has no object at all—The esthetic enjoyment is not the enjoyment of an object, but the enjoyment of self. It is an immediate feeling of value that is lodged in oneself. This feeling is not a feeling that is related to an object;-
>
> Ex. – There is no separation in it between my pleased ego and that with which I am pleased, in it both are one and the same self, the immediately experienced ego.
>
> On the other hand, in aesthetic enjoyment, the sense of value may be objectified. - In contemplating the strong, free, proud human form standing before me, I do not feel strong, proud and free as such, or in my own place, or in my own body, but feel myself thus in the contemplated form and only in it.[18]

Aesthetic enjoyment is then: (1) the enjoyment of an object, which, so long as it is the object of enjoyment, is not an object, but the individual ego, or (2) it is the enjoyment of the ego, which, inasmuch as it is aesthetically enjoyed, is not the ego, but is the self objectified. This is to say that the feelings which accompany aesthetic contemplation are not only those of enjoyment, but that the individual also feels himself. For this reason, these subjective qualities may be attributed to any object, for

> ...they belong and with them the self, or the self belongs, and with it these qualities, to that object with which the individual feels himself and his subjective states inextricably bound, whenever he stops to contemplate the object.[19]

Aesthetic pleasure derives from the ease with which the ego adjusts in response to the aesthetic stimulus. Ideally, when the observer is presented with the external object, he responds immediately with a mentally imagined self-activity, experiencing a loss of consciousness as he feels himself into the object. Aesthetic pleasure, then, is pleasure in the perceived object, but not in the object as such, but only insomuch as the individual has felt himself into it. Both aesthetic enjoyment and pleasure, as formerly illustrated, involved the activity of forces and projection of the ego, and have as their aim a well integrated attitude. It may be concluded that creative discovery is the source of such an aesthetic experience.

As evidenced in Lipps' writings there are three traits of the aesthetic experience:

1. Isolation—The aesthetic experience is complete in itself and does not direct the individual's attention to anything outside itself.

2. Unity—The individual successfully adjusts to the activity and does not desire to alter the aesthetic object's composition in any way.
3. Significance—The experience is charged with life and meaning and possesses a real and present import.20

As formerly mentioned, the aesthetic experience occurs when the individual enters into the object in full compliance with the movement it implies. The attention is then focalized and held on the object, and imagination dominates the entire individual consciousness at this time. Since the individual is at one with the ego, he possesses a new identity. Lipps describes this as being released from our own consciousness, and consequently, absorbed in the object of art. It appears then that the aesthetic experience is an interaction in time between mind and object, and that the contemplator enters into a certain kind of relationship with the aesthetic object. Such an experience is characterized not only by the aforementioned isolation and unity, but also involves the total self. Because of this the perceived object possesses a richer quality and takes on the character of deep significance. Ironically, one of the critics of Lipps' aesthetic theory, Martin Buber, has given an even more exact definition:

> Empathy means...to glide with one's own feeling into the dynamic structure of an object, a pillar, or a crystal or the branch of a tree, or even of an animal or a man, and as it were to trace it from within, understanding the formation and motoriality of the object with the perception of one's own imagination, it means to "transpose" oneself over there and in there.21

As previously indicated empathy to Lipps was a metaphysical projection of the ego. The inner activity or striving was viewed as a purely mental process without any sensational basis. In this sense empathy simply represents the disappearance of the two-fold consciousness of self and object. Consequently, in contemplating the aesthetic object, the individual is free from actual experience of physiological processes. Instead he is involved in the science of the mind and of mental phenomena. Lipps purposely designated his interpretation of empathy imaginative as a protest to the emphasis being placed on psyiological factors by scientific esthetics. In the same manner he defended his theory by criticizing the disease of preoccupation with sense feelings which he felt to be prevalent in his time. The concept of empathy as a mystical substance of the mind distinguishes Lipps' writings from all other empathy theorists, and the theory is widely employed in aesthetic circles.

The Kinesthetic Theory of Empathy

A second theory of empathy is known as kinesthetic, or motor empathy, and places an emphasis on organic sensations and bodily positions. Vernon Lee first published an account of the process in 1897 in an article, "Beauty and Ugliness," which appeared in the *Contemporary Review*. Because exponents of this school interpret perception in terms of sensory activities and processes, the kinesthetic theory originated as a reaction to Lipps' view of empathy as a metaphysical projection of the ego. The following areas have been systematically examined:

1. Types of Movement
2. Kinesthetic sensations in relation to motor movement
3. Kinesthetic empathy in relation to preception
4. Kinesthetic empathy as a determining factor of the aesthetic experience

Types of Movement

In sharp contrast to Lipps' theory of empathy as a mystical substance of the mind, kinesthetic writers favor the theory of "inner mimicry." Consequently, they agree that motor mimicry is present in the following relationships:

1. Person-to-person relationship: The individual tends to mimic the movements of another person or persons.
2. Person-to-object relationship: The individual responds kinesthetically to the tensions or feelings aroused by an object or objects.

In person-to-person mimicry the individual actually imitates the gestures and movements of the other person. As a result his own muscles and physical postures undergo certain changes. Watching a basketball game, the individual may feel himself a part of the action of the court and contract his own muscles as the guard leaps upward to make a basket; he may also respond to the excitement of the game by participating in the physical tensions of the crowd; - when they jump up to cheer, he jumps to his feet. In responding to the contagious excitement of the event the individual thereby becomes one with the feelings and actions of his neighbors. Similarly, when we are passengers in a car we press on the floor as the driver attempts to pass another vehicle; as we watch the action on a high trapeze, our own muscles become taut and rigid; when we attend a boxing match, we impute physical blows to the participants; our bodies lean in the direction in which the ball is being carried at a football game; and we find ourselves swaying to and fro as we respond to the motion of dancers, or to the gliding of a group of skaters. In person-to-person mimicry the individual may be said to co-experience the movement of another person or persons through the process of spontaneous imitation. The end result is that the individual becomes correspondingly active in the same way.

Motor mimicry in a person-to-object relationship occurs when the individual experiences certain inner sensations as he views a certain object or objects. Such inner activity is possible because the sight of the object arouses the memory of former movements, or because the object arouses some tension or feeling in the muscles. For example, if an individual were to observe a boulder, he might imagine himself raising or attempting to raise it. This would elicit kinesthetic sensations, and these might arouse the memory of having lifted heavy objects in the past as well as the effect of the experience. Consequently, a sensation of heaviness is felt in the observer. The question then is not whether or not the boulder is heavy, but that the sensation of heaviness is felt. Hypothetically an individual might say that one object appears heavy while another light, when in actuality they are both heavy. Through this process of association and motor adjustment the individual is enabled to experience the object's space, weight, form, smoothness, delicacy, and other such related factors.

Person-to-object mimicry, like person-to-person mimicry, centers around the idea of motor responses and muscular reactions. As such, kinesthetic empathy signifies the acting out of a represented action. One can easily see that the theory is in direct contrast to Lipps' concept of empathy as the subtle imitation of form and line.

Kinesthetic Sensations in Realtion to Motor Movement

It is agreed that "sense feelings" refer to the feelings localized in the body; to kinesthetic sensations and motor responses. Kinesthetic theorists acknowledge that the feelings connected with bodily actions and muscular movements are largely unconscious. This is illustrated by the fact that when we listen to music we subconsciously move in time to the rhythm. Similarly we have the tendency to imitate the notes in a corresponding fashion in the throat, and in silent reading we sometimes automatically move the lips or muscles of the larynx. In aesthetic contemplation then, the movements do not come to consciousness as sensations within the body, but these bodily processes are imputed instead to the object. This means that the force of lines and figures is, in actuality, the inner activity of the individual. The fact that there are kinesthetic responses is not known by the individual at the time of the experience, but is recognized only by later reflection. In this respect the exponents specify that there can be no coalescence of movements with the line, no fusion of the sensations with the object, as long as attention is consciously directed to the kinesthetic process. The favored formula of perception then is not "I feel roundness or symmetry," but rather "the object is round, or uniform, or balanced." In terms of the kinesthetic theory it may be concluded that the physiological response of the individual supposedly becomes more objectified and, hence, unconscious as it merges in the activity of the perceptive process.

The Significance of Kinesthetic Empathy in Relation to Perception

Adherents of the kinesthetic theory assert that sensations have no meaning in themselves and that they are an incorporated part of the process of perception. They further acknowledge that all perceptions are dependent upon the motor attitudes that are assumed toward the object. This being the case, it is necessary to explore fully the role of motor response in relation to perception. One interpretation is that motor mimicry is a means of understanding other people. From this standpoint, the basic quality of empathy is spontaneous imitation. Abraham Luchins, in discussing the value of mimicry in person-to-person relationships, theorizes that empathy is possible because facial and bodily events correspond to the inner mental activity.[22] Phrased slightly differently, the way a person inwardly feels is evidenced in his overt activity. Accordingly, through imitating this overt behavior, the observer experiences an understanding of the other person. Equally as important in evoking appropriate moods, however, is person-to-object mimicry. In this respect the individual is said to experience static objects through the process of inner mimicry. Such movement specifically enables him to realize the true distance of the object from him, its space, weight, form, quality of touch, and other such related features. That the motor response is an instrumental factor in empathic situations, is thus affirmed by the kinesthetic theorists. The same theorists also acknowledge that an analysis of the motor attitude assumed in person-to-object mimicry increases the observer's future participation in such events. Significantly, through an examination of his own "muscle knowledge," the individual will be able to expand the richness of the immediate experience, intensify the critical function, and in fact, heighten the power of designation.

Kinesthetic Empathy as a Determining Factor of the Aesthetic Experience

As set forth by the kinesthetic theory, the aesthetic experience is the result of of the individual's unified and organized adjustment into the object. There are two forms of adjustment which may be made in regard to an object, one of which relates to the aesthetic experience, the other not. The one is an adjustment toward, the other an adjustment in. When one sees a weeping willow tree swaying in the breeze, he may adopt a motor attitude which tries to stop the motion, or he may have the impulse to sway with the weeping willow and thus perceive the true nature of its motion. Similarly two adjustments may be made toward the outstretched hand of a statue: either one of squeezing the hand, or secondly, of feeling the "outstretching" of the hand. It is the latter type of adjustment which is favored by these theorists. Supposedly the individual's inner feelings are no longer repressed and denied when he makes this adjustment, and the subjective configurations are clearly perceived as belonging to the object of perception. The kinesthetic empathizer also responds to the aesthetic experience as an incomplete whole seeking higher integration, he is in a state of being. It follows that a situation is said to be beautiful when the individual achieves the proper bodily attitude. The resulting effect is an experience of heightened vitality.[23]

The kinesthetic theory of empathy is in direct contrast to Lipps' view of empathy as a purely mental activity, or metaphsical projection of the ego. The main feature then stresses kinesthetic sensations and muscular adjustments. That every variety and degree of motion which occurs during the perception process has aesthetic significance may be said to be the basis for the kinesthetic interpretation of empathy.

THE ROLE OF EMPATHY IN RELATION TO THE FIELD OF ORAL INTERPRETATION

The preceding psychological and philosophical principals of empathy which have been described in Part I and II pertain to art theory and to empathy as an ingredient of aesthetic response. The particular significance and value of empathy in oral interpretation has been recognized by various authorities in the field. A brief summary of their treatment of the concept is as follows:

1. The Nature of Empathy — Discussions relating to empathy and the empathic process.
2. The Meaning of Empathy - Considerations of the two major theories of empathy, the Lipps Theory and the Kinesthetic Theory, and their appropriateness to the art of oral interpretation.
3. The Uses of Empathy — The function of empathy in relation to literature, the oral interpreter, and communicator-communicatee effectiveness.

In order to examine properly the role of empathy in relation to oral interpretation, it is necessary that these findings be compared and evaluated with the theories previously described in Part I and Part II.

THE NATURE OF EMPATHY

The Empathic Response

Many writers in oral interpretation favor the role of experience as an instrumental factor in the individual's empathic response. Such a viewpoint is valid in that empathy consists of self-revelations, or knowledge about what is innately one's own. In this respect the storehouse of experience which each reader brings to the interpretive act is indeed valuable. However, it must be remembered that the interpreter's task is more than that of simply interpreting his own experience. His function, in contrast, is that of interpreting the word symbols of other men's experiences. Of necessity, the concept of empathy thus implies far more than an analogy with personal experience. This is to say that, hypothetically, even if the individual does not know "how it is" (the experience he is to represent), through the use of empathy he may imaginatively conjecture "how it must be." Consequently the role of experience provides only a partial explanation of the empathic response. It remains that the phenomenon's great strength is that it yields information about what is foreign or outside the individual.

In addition to the view of empathy as an experiential response, various textbook writers also characterize empathic response as a particular type of reaction. From this standpoint the diligent reader is thereby admonished to give unstintingly of himself so that the thrill of communication can occur, the strength of the thrill being determined by the amount of the *bodily* processes which take place. However, except for the mention of bodily processes, there is a general failure to specifically distinguish the kind of reaction involved. We see the confusion illustrated further in that one group of authors contends that the empathic response is spontaneous and unconscious, another group implies that it is conscious and subject to the will, and a third group favors a combination of both. In defining the empathic response as a physical sensation, it may correctly be said that the individual's activity is full of significance. Such activity may be deemed significant, however, only to the extent that the individual's movements are *attributed to the object of perception* and absorbed therein. Indeed, the empathic individual is the one who is released from his own counsciousness. Instead of equating the empathic response with motor reaction per se, perhaps a more valid definition would be a consideration of empathic response as an interactional process which involves the transmission of knowledge and feeling.

The Aesthetic Experience

At the beginning of this chapter it was asserted that empathy can be used to engender a reader-writer-audience communion of experience so that enjoyment and appreciation may be fully shared. In relation to the oral interpretation act this means that the literature, the reader, and the audience are all actively involved in the artistic creation. The aesthetic experience thus is the projection of transposition of one's self over and into an imaginative experience. In this regard many of the oral interpretation theorists have directed most of their attention to the results of the experience, the aesthetic effect. One finds that the effect is not only described in terms of organic sensations but is also vaguely represented as being "quite an experience." Very little consideration is given to the variables, or states of being, involved in the aesthetic experience. Consequently, as one searches the texts, the only alternative is that of conjecture. For example, does the aesthetic experience have pattern and structure? – is there a single quality which pervades the entire experience – is the aesthetic experience complete in itself? If there are answers, our literature fails to supply them at this particular time. For two reasons there needs to be differentiation concerning the state of being during empathic experience: (1) because the aesthetic experience is an interaction in time between mind and object, and (2) because the individual enters into a particular kind of relationship with the object. An understanding of the aesthetic experience is necessary because it will improve the interpreter's chief function - that of reproducing the essential life of the work for a shared communion of response.

THE MEANING OF EMPATHY

Those in oral interpretation acknowledge the existence of the two major theories of empathy which have previously been discussed, the Lipps Theory and the Kinesthetic Theory. For the most part the latter theory is preferred, and thus the empathic process is characterized as one involving motor responses and muscular reactions. Very little attention is given to Lipps' concept of empathy as a purely mental activity. In employing the physiological approach many writers, however, do not distinguish the empathic process from other bodily processes. For example, this writer has even seen empathy discussed under such categories as bodily action and gesture. Rather than penetrating the significance of empathy, it appears that these writers have dwelt on minutiae instead.

Taken singularly, motor mimicry is an inexact definition of empathy, for it must be remembered that empathy comprises not one, but several dimensions. In subscribing primarily to the kinesthetic approach many in the field have overlooked the probability that the relation between what is done and what is undergone in the empathic response varies from individual to individual. Furthermore, because the majority of oral interpretation exponents have favored this particular type of empathy, all possible viewpoints have not been considered. It appears that such a limited approach can only impede the full understanding of empathy.

THE USES OF EMPATHY

Empathy in Relation
to Literature

In their literary analyses, oral interpretation writers have differentiated between the thinking ("cognitive") and feeling ("affective") aspects of a work. In terms of empathy this distinction has led to a primary emphasis on the emotive aspects of literature. The result is an implication that the emotional or evocative language of a work serves as the key to the intended empathic response. However, to the interpreter, who must know his intended effect, this can prove misleading. For example, in fully expressing the dimensions of the text, the interpreter must remember that the internal complex rests on an intellectual as well as emotional foundation. No literary work is ever completely "emotional," nor is it ever to be considered solely "intellectual." Rather the two are intertwined, and the empathic experience may be viewed as a fusion of these two elements. Therefore, both the cognitive and affective ingredients of the work must be treated in order that the dimensions of the performance equal the actual thoughts and feelings of the text. It would appear that oral interpretation writers have emphasized empathy's value in the "transmission of feeling" and have failed to give proper consideration to the concept's equivalent value in the "transmission of knowledge."

Empathy in Relation to
the Oral Interpreter

In their discussions of empathy and the oral interpreter, writers have again stressed kinesthetic sensations and muscular movements. Their viewpoint is that the degree of empathy can be spotted by noting the outer physical changes of the interpreter. This particular viewpoint, however, should be re-examined for two reasons. First of all, as was mentioned in the first two sections, the relation between what is done and what is undergone in empathy varies among individuals. Secondly, it is fallacious to unduly emphasize particular aspects of the empathic response rather than the total response. The writers, for the most part, also make little or no mention of the psychological research on empathic ability which was discussed in the earlier portion of this chapter. It would seem that these findings could well be used as guidelines, for the major consideration should be how the oral interpreter can use empathy to translate a set of symbols, the literature, into a meaningful experience for both reader and listeners.

Empathy in Relation to
Communicator-Communicatee Effectiveness

The role of the reader and that of the audience is one of communicative participation. In their discussions of the audience, many writers in the field have equated the circular response with overt action and movement. The inference in this respect is two-fold: (1) the oral reader's movement is necessary because it stimulates the listeners to respond empathically, and (2) the audience will mimic the suggestion of overt movement provided by the interpreter, such mimicry being a sign of the degree of empathy present in the situation. It is misleading, however, to assume that the oral interpreter-audience relationship is one in which the former directs the empathic response of the latter by superimposing his (the interpreter's) bodily responses. On the contrary, the interpreter cannot transmit responses, he can only use empathy as a means of catalyzing or stirring up responses. From the standpoint of the audience then it may be said that empathic response is personal and individual. Assuredly it is much more than overt mimicry. More importantly, in judging the circular response activity of the audience, allowance must be made for covert reactions and mentally imagined responses. Instead of employing an observational listener-reader mimicry scale in judging the degree of empathy present, perhaps a more valid approach for those in oral interpretation is as follows: Empathy comprises a continuum of subtle nuances of feeling and thought and is a process which, in terms of audience considerations, cannot be measured solely by the tangible display of expression.

This chapter has been an attempt to consider empathy and its relation to aesthetic experience and oral interpretation. Basic research may be traced to psychology, for there are few investigations of empathy in relation to oral interpretation. There is no general agreement by those in the field of oral interpretation on the nature and meaning of empathy, although concensus is reached on the fact that empathy implies a transmission of knowledge and feeling. Opinions vary, however, regarding the exact procedure involved in the empathic process. Consequently, no separate and specific reaction has been defined and descriptions of the empathic process are often vague and misleading. Because of the prevailing tendency of oral interpretation exponents to subscribe to one particular theory of empathy, the Kinesthetic Theory, all possible viewpoints have not been considered. Such an approach has seemingly negated the free spirit of inquiry, and thus, a full understanding of empathy is impeded. Presently a broader perspective by those in oral interpretation is needed in order that the full dimensions of the empathic process be realized. Altogether, literary re-creation and appreciation suggest fascinating problems which someday might be solved through proper attention to the phenomenon of empathy.

FOOTNOTES

[1]A notable exception is Chloe Armstrong and Paul D. Brandes, *The Oral Interpretation of Literature* (New York: McGraw-Hill Book Co., Inc., 1963).

[2]For a full explanation see Joyce Horton, "A Study of Empathy and its Relation to Aesthetic Experience and Oral Interpretation." Unpublished Master's thesis (Auburn University, 1965), pp. 15-36.

[3]David Stewart,*Preface to Empathy* (New York: Philosophical Library, 1956), p. 5.

[4]Robert L. Katz,*Empathy: Its Nature and Uses* (Glencoe: Free Press, 1963), p. 64.

[5]Sigmund Freud,*Civilization and Its Discontents.*In the Standard Edition. Vol. XXI. Edited by James Strachey (London: Hogarth Press, 1961 [1930]), p. 68.

[6]Ethelyn Pearson, "Empathy Unlimited,"*Writer,* LXXVI (February, 1963), p. 25.

[7]Irving Lorge, "The Psychologist's Contribution to the Communication of Idea," *The Communication of Idea.,*ed. Lyman Bryson (New York: 1948), p. 83.

[8]H. A. Overstreet,*The Mature Mind* (New York: W. W. Norton and Co., 1950), p. 65.

[9]Stewart, op. cit., p. 47.

[10]Gregory Zilboorg, (in collaboration with George W. Henry) *A History of Medical Psychology* (New York: Norton, 1941), p. 18.

[11]Paul Federn, *Ego Psychology and the Psychoses* (New York: Basic Books, 1952), p. 344.

[12]Walter Jackson Bates,*From Classic to Romantic* (Cambridge, Mass: Harvard University Press, 1956), p. 143.

[13]The four theories are discussed at length in this writer's thesis. Horton, op. cit., pp. 52-124.

[14]Lipps further amplifies and illustrates his concept of empathy in a series of essays published in *Psychologische Untersuchungen,* Theodor Lipps, ed. (Leipzig,1912), II, in toto.

[15]For a description of these findings see Christian A. Ruckmick,*Psychology of Feeling and Emotion.* 1st edition (New York: McGraw-Hill Book Co., 1936), p. 147.

[16]Robert Vischer,*Drei Schriften zum aesthetischen Formproblem* (Halle, 1927), p. 26.

[17]Theodore Lipps, "Empathy, Inner Imitation, and Sense Feelings,"*A Modern Book of Esthetics*, ed. Melvin M. Rader (New York: Henry Holt and Co., 1935), pp. 295-301.

[18]*Ibid.,*p.. 293.

[19]*Ibid.,* p. 295.

[20]Lipps,*op. cit., Psychologische Untersuchungen.*

[21]Martin Buber, *Between Man and Man.* Translated by Ronald Gregor Smith (New York: Macmillan, 1948), p. 97.

[22]Abraham Luchins, "A Variational Approach to Empathy," *Journal of Social Psychology,* XXXXV, No. 1 (1957), pp. 113-119.

[23]For a complete description of kinesthetic empathy see Vernon Lee, "Empathy."*A Modern Book of Esthetics.* Edited by Melvin M. Rader (New York: Henry Holt and Co., 1935), pp. 305-310.

FURTHER READINGS

ART THEORY

Langfeld,Harold Sidney, *The Aesthetic Attitude.* Harcourt, Brace & World, Inc., New York, 1920.

Mundt, K., "Three Aspects of German Aesthetic Theory," *Journal of Aesthetics and Art Criticism,* XVII. March 1959, pp. 287-310.

Philipson, Morriss, *Aesthetics Today.* World Publishing Company, Cleveland, 1961.

Rader, Melvin M., (ed.), *A Modern Book of Esthetics.* Henry Holt & Company, New York, 1935.

Sparshott,F. E., *The Structure of Aesthetics.* University of Toronto Press, Toronto, 1963.

Vivas, Eliseo and Murray Krieger, (ed.), *The Problems of Aesthetics.* Holt, Rinehart & Winston, New York, 1963.

PSYCHOLOGICAL RESEARCH

Becker, Howard, "Empathy, Sympathy and Scheler, *International Journal of Sociometry,* I, No. 1. 1956, pp. 15-22.

Bell, G. B., and Rhoda Stolper, "An Attempt at Validation of the Empathy Test, *Journal of Applied Psychology,* XXXIX. December, 1955, pp. 442-43.

Buchheimer, Arnold, "The Development of Ideas About Empathy," *Journal of Counseling Psychology,* X. Spring, 1963, pp. 61-70.

Cottrell, L. S., and Rosaline F. Dymond, "The Empathic Responses: A Neglected Field for Research,*Psychiatry,* XII, No. 4. 1949, pp. 355-59.

Dymond, R. F., "A Preliminary Investigation of the Relation of Insight and Empathy," *Journal of Consulting Psychology,* XII. July, 1948, pp. 228-33.

___,"A Scale for the Measurement of Emphatic Ability," *Journal of Consulting Psychology,* XIII. April, 1949, pp. 127-33.

___,"Personality and Empathy," *Journal of Consulting Psychology,* XIV. 1950, pp. 343-50.

Hastorf, A. H., and I. E. Bender, "A Caution Respecting the Measurement of Empathic Ability," *Journal of Abnormal and Social Psychology,* XXXXVII. 1952, pp. 574-76.

Norman, Ralph D., and Patricia Ainsworth, "The Relationship Among Projection, Empathy, Reality and Adjustment Operationally Defined," *Journal of Consulting Psychology,* XVIII, No. 1. 1954, pp. 53-58.

Norman,Ralph D., and Waldemar C. Leiding, "The Relationship Between Measures of Individual and Mass Empathy," *Journal of Consulting Psychology,* XX, No. 1. 1956, pp. 79-82.

Toomer, Laura Carolyn, "Factors Affecting Empathic Performance." Unpublished Ph. D. dissertation, University of Connecticut, 1962.

Chapter VII

THE CRITICISM: IN TEACHING ORAL INTERPRETATION

Martin Cobin

Criticism plays a vital role in oral interpretation. This chapter discusses the basic nature of the critical function and offers suggestions concerning evaluating and guiding the oral interpreter.

In this discussion of criticism I shall attempt to perform but two tasks: (1) set forth concepts I consider to be so fundamental and indispensable that they demand inclusion; and (2) suggest attitudes that may be sufficiently divergent to be provocative. With respect to the second task, I hope to avoid sophistry by restricting myself to those divergent opinions that appeal to me, not so much because of their provocativeness as because of the firmness with which I believe them to be valid. At the risk of undue complexity, I shall try to approach both tasks with a sensitivity to the points of view of the teacher, the student, and the scholar. I shall not attempt to reflect these different viewpoints in any formal presentational pattern; the reader can choose from his own orientation, whatever seems pertinent.

THE CRITICAL FUNCTION

Criticism, in its fullest sense, includes analysis, evaluation, and guidance. Analysis can be, and frequently is, undertaken independently of criticism; but criticism cannot be freed from a dependence upon analysis without becoming so amorphous as to be merely intuitive. Obviously many of us, frequently, and probably all of us, occasionally, are critically active on an intuitive level; this is often necessary and useful for the simple reason that we must make decisions based on our evaluations and in response to our desires for improvement even when we lack the time, the tools, or the technical ability to engage in objective analysis. The degree to which we are forced to use primitive methods, however, does not alter the fact of their primitiveness or the probability of their relative ineffectiveness. If we admit the merits of emergency measures, we should continue to employ these measures only in emergencies. It is helpful, in this regard, to be quite clear in our identification of the emergency measures. Similarly, it is helpful—when we identify critical activity on an intuitive level—to recognize it as something quite distinct from full-blown criticism. If we are clear in making this distinction, we should then insist on seeking the greater rewards of criticism whenever there are available to us the necessary time, tools, and

* Portions reprinted from *Western Speech*, Winter, 1964 by permission of Western Speech Association.

techniques. More specifically, we should include in our perceptions of criticism the time, tools, and techniques of analysis; so that we evaluate and offer guidance on the basis of an objective awareness of what exists and what does not exist.

To the extent that the analytic basis for criticism is objective (and effective) it is relatively independent of the analyst—or, in this case, the analyst-critic. That is, the analytical procedures should be capable of clear delineation and, when applied by different critics (or by the same critic at different times), should yield comparable results. This dimension of criticism has several significant implications. First, it suggests the necessity for the critic to articulate his analytical procedures so that others can assess the validity of the data-collecting upon which he bases his evaluations and his prescriptions for improvement. Second, it suggests that his data-collecting procedures can be tested for reliability—by himself or by others—by simply determining whether they actually yield comparable results when employed by different people or on different occasions.

The situation is quite different with respect to both evaluation (the determination of the good and the poor) and guidance (the facilitation of improvement). Neither of these critical functions has meaning independent of the critic. However objective the critic may seek to be in these matters, his subjective judgments and values necessarily are involved in evaluation; his total personality necessarily affects both his choice of procedures of guidance and the effectiveness of those procedures. The cultural complex within which the critic functions will also influence his judgments, his values, his personality, his perceptions of available procedures, and the response of others to both his personality and his procedures. The student or practitioner who seeks to benefit from criticism may well profit from a conscious awareness of the degree to which the criticism is necessarily affected by the nature of the critic. Likewise, the critic who is a teacher will profit from realizing that the criticism he expresses within the framework of a specific teaching environment is necessarily affected by his philosophy of education. Just as any meaningful consideration of criticism must include the critic, any meaningful consideration of criticism in education must include the personality and educational philosophy of the teacher-critic. For example, I know some teachers contentedly working within an educational environment stressing the professional development of highly gifted students. I know other teachers equally contented in an educational environment chiefly concerned with the general cultural development of students possessing no unique talents in the teacher's area of primary interest. I know teachers who can make students laugh at their own errors with honest enjoyment of the humor involved and with a keen appreciation of the teacher's depth of concern for the student as a person. I know other teachers who cannot joke with students without the jokes becoming barbed and the students demoralized. I would not suggest, therefore, that any single procedure for criticism is equally applicable to all critics in all circumstances.

Evaluation is a matter of discriminating among the superior, the good, the mediocre, and the inadequate. This discrimination serves two educational purposes—it helps establish standards and it provides a basis for improvement. The student cannot work effectively to improve unless he knows his strengths and his weaknesses and unless he knows the difference between one level of ability and another. The student is a learner among learners. He cannot always trust his own feeling of what is right; nor can he always trust the responses of his peers who share his own lack of sensitivity and his own limited or non-existent contact with excellence. The ability of the teacher-critic to supply the proper responses does not result from any magical properties that come automatically with his position. The teacher-critic can provide significant evaluation only to the extent that he himself is sensitive and only to the extent that he has had numerous contacts with excellence.

The ability to move on from evaluation to the constructive task of helping the student (or practitioner) improve is dependent on a keen analytical sense and on the capacity to communicate what analysis reveals. It is also dependent on a thoroughgoing technical knowledge that will provide the storehouse from which insights and possibilities may be drawn. The good teacher does not provide answers, only questions; but the answers must be known—at least in a general sense—before the proper questions can be asked. The dull or the egocentric teacher provides answers and limits the creativity of the student. The dishonest or unqualified teacher asks questions not from choice but from necessity; and in the process he often asks the wrong questions and discredits himself, his discipline, and his profession.

There is, appropriately, considerable concern as to the manner of giving criticism, of announcing the evaluation, and of going about the process of facilitating improvement. What is vital here is not a set of rules but a personal orientation. The teacher-critic must be dedicated to his field and he must respect the inherent worth and human dignity of his students. The teacher who manifests this dedication and this respect is free to break any rule in the book of critique etiquette.

Before turning to specific applications in oral interpretation, I believe there will be value in considering two more aspects of the critical function. One of these concerns the teacher-student relationship within the modern context of education. The other relates to the dilemma of the scholar-critic.

Contemporary education is becoming progressively (although in many cases reluctantly and slowly) less concerned with the teacher's role as a conveyor of information and more concerned with the educator's role as a creator of specific types of learning situations. It is not clear, nor for our purposes need it be, as to whether this change primarily results from altered perceptions of educational theory or whether the theorizing itself is a response to the explosion of knowledge which has resulted in quantities of information obviously too vast to be conveyed to the student within the available period of training. The pressures imposed on the educational system are apparent in any field (and there are many) in which a lifetime of study is too brief a time span, for the simple reason that new information is being obtained faster than the individual can learn. Of necessity, then, education objectives must either be abandoned as impossibilities or re-defined. The third alternative (which is obvious, totally inadequate, and unfortunately if understandably prevalent) is to maintain the old objective of conveying information as if the information were, in fact, of a nature and a quantity that could be taught and learned. Where the most productive re-definition has occurred, however, it has taken the form of seeking to give the student a core of information, a skill in manipulating this information, and a motivation to manipulate it so as to achieve whatever additional information he subsequently finds personally or socially useful. A helpful analogy would be to compare the objective of teaching a student everything that could be known about a small geographical area, with a new objective of teaching him what he needed to know to be able to find his way and survive in an area so vast that he could not traverse or come to know all of it in a lifetime of travel and exploration. This discussion is not a digression; it should be apparent that this re-definition of objective in large part may be described, quite meaningfully, as a decision to develop the critical function of the student— the ability to analyze for the purpose of evaluation and improvement.

At this point, the critic seems on the verge of claiming a social utility of tremendous significance, a utility which is a response to the knowledge explosion created by the new methods or technologies of investigation. This very revolution in technology, however, has infused the scholar with an overpowering commitment to objectivity. This commitment, in turn, has led the scholar-critic to focus on that phase of criticism which gives greatest scope to objectivity and to turn away from those aspects of criticism which are most tainted by subjectivity. As a consequence, criticism in general, and scholarly criticism in particular, has been abandoning the evaluative and corrective function and restricting itself more and more exclusively to the analytical function. In doing so, the critic has become more firmly entrenched as a source of a particular kind of information, and simultaneously, less frequently perceived as dealing with information of any real pertinence to the major concerns of humanity.

To return to the previous analogy, the critic is like the guide who, in a period of growing need for people to lead groups through the forest, concentrates more and more on improving his ability to traverse the six square miles of particular interest to him—a progressively less useful response to social needs as the distance to be traversed in the forest extends farther and farther beyond the number of square mile tracts that can be included within the interests of the total number of available guides. What I am suggesting here is that the scholar-critic has been particularly negligent in failing to perceive the larger social context to which he could be applying his processes. He has failed to perceive this because of his response to a technology which, in the very period of distorting the scholar-critic's focus, is creating an increasing need for the contributions of the well-oriented scholar-critic. I believe another manifestation of this is the tendency of many of those critics who accept the evaluative function to limit their evaluations to matters of form (or style) as distinguished, most carefully, from content. Here again it can be asserted that scholarly objectivity is much more readily maintained with respect to form than with respect to content; but also that the social need of the critical function is more related to that analysis which seeks to provide a basis for evaluations and improvements of style only in terms of content. To return to the familiar analogy, the guide should check the apparel of his party of travelers not with respect to the standards of latest fashion, but in terms of the travel conditions to be met in reaching the desired destination; similarly, he must select a destination in terms of the needs of the travelers and not merely to increase the chances of a quick, easy journey which will reflect well—at least initially—upon his own efficiency.

ORAL INTERPRETATION

The work of the interpreter must be evaluated in terms of its function. The function concept is perceived, all too often, in an overly restrictive manner. Interpretation is not the "recitation of pieces" that it often appears to be within the drill context of many elementary interpretation courses. It is, rather, the speech delivery of literary materials designed either to enrich the life of the listener through the art-response experience involved, or to serve as a vehicle for the communicative objective of interpreter-speaker. In other words, the function may be primarily interpretative or primarily creative. I have chosen these terms deliberately, in full consciousness of the fact that interpretation and creativity are involved in both functions and that the implied dichotomy may be irritating. I believe it is necessary, however, to recognize quite frankly the difference that exists between these two functions.

The interpretative function leaves the interpreter as a middle-man between the literature and the audience. The evaluation of this function focuses on the extent to which the interpreter is responsive to the literature and the extent to which he stimulates a comparable responsiveness in his audience. Guidance, similarly, focuses on increasing the student's sensitivity to the literature and perfecting his capacity to excite the sensibilities of his audience. It is in relation to this function that teachers have developed the multi-faceted and multi-labeled techniques of impression and expression—ranging through the whole continuum from the expression-centered "platform performers" to the impression centered "literary scholars" and including the advocates of varying degrees of proportioning and balancing the extremes.

The creative function places on the interpreter-speaker the burden of formulating the communicative purpose and of selecting literary materials that will serve as vehicles for the accomplishment of this purpose. The focus of evaluation here is on the significance of the insights and communicative objectives of the speaker, the pertinence of his selection of literary materials, and the skill with which these materials are integrated into the communicative effort—both in conception and in speech delivery. The focus of guidance, then, is on developing the student's motivation to exploit his full capacity as a human being, increasing his knowledge of literature with a resultant increase in his ability to choose appropriate materials, and improving his communicative skill both as a speaker and as an interpretative reader.

Perhaps at least one high-sounding goal should be related to a few specific techniques for achieving it—just to establish the fact that my brevity is deliberate rather than merely an inevitable product of vagueness. How can the teacher develop the student's motivation to exploit his full capacity as a human being? Or, to take at least one major dimension of this, how can the teacher create in the student (or the critic create in the practitioner) a desire to say something of significance? First, the student must know what significance is. This is facilitated by examples and by discussion. Second, the student must become aware of his own capacity to say something significant. This is facilitated by involving the student in discussions of significant topics that relate to the student and by dealing with his contributions to that discussion in terms of their significance. Third, the student must come to appreciate the value of interpretation as a powerful means of helping to express something of significance. This, too, is facilitated by example and by discussion. Fourth, the student must experience the satisfaction that comes with personal success in the communication of significant ideas. This is facilitated by careful and thorough coaching. It may be objected that I have not yet defined "significance" in any precise terms. I admit that such is the case but I refuse to acknowledge that my failure is objectionable. The nature of significance must be defined by each teacher for himself just as—in the last analysis—it must be defined by each individual for himself. What I describe here as approaches to motivating a concern for significance has a breadth of applicability just to the degree that the reader can accept it independent of his ability to accept my own, or any other, specific definition of significance.

In the four points of the preceding paragraph, I have mentioned three key concepts: example, discussion, and coaching. The real value of thorough coaching lies in its contribution to the student's achievement of a communicative experience that would otherwise not be available to him at the current stage of his development. The coach's long-range objective is neither to push the student through a doorway nor to carry him through it but to open the door and reveal something so exciting that the student wants to get through on his own. Some pushing and carrying may be appropriate; but when the coaching creates a student attitude of "I'm lazy, push me!" or "I'm malleable, shape me!" the coaching has failed. The value of example is more fully realized when it is supplied frequently. Recordings and the work of other students can often supply examples. The teacher must be prepared to supply examples as well. The value of discussion is best realized through a classroom activity too often neglected by teachers of interpretation–probing the audience response to the ideas and the feelings, to the shared experience rather than to the techniques of the interpreter's presentation. Students in an interpretation class should not be shocked if, after hearing an essay or a public address interpreted to them, the teacher asks, "Do you agree?"

The interpreter's preparation will differ, depending on whether the function is interpretative or creative. The differences are self-evident. The phase of preparation common to both functions is the oral reading of the literature. I have nothing to add here to what is readily available concerning the techniques of impression. I do feel the need, with regard to expression (or what I would prefer to call communication), to insist that technique has as legitimate a place in the art of interpretation as in any art. The techniques of art *are* artificial. In this regard, the purpose of preparation is to master the technical applications to the point where they become so easily handled as to appear natural and, therefore, to go unnoticed. Such preparation can be achieved effectively, however, only by spending time in conscious and deliberate attention to the techniques. The evaluation of the student who is practicing his interpretation and the guidance given to him during his practice sessions should reflect the teacher-critic's awareness of this vital phase of preparation.

Presentation should never take place without evaluation and guidance. I believe the social awareness of this constitutes the basis for the existence of criticism in any culture with highly developed arts. In the narrower context of formal education, I am inclined to think that interpretative presentation in the classroom generally suffers from two deficiencies: it is too frequent and it is too limited in conception. When I say it is too frequent, I mean that it takes up classroom time that could be more advantageously used for preparation. This relates to criticism because the slighting of preparation in the classroom frequently stems from the teacher's reluctance to deal openly and in detail with delivery techniques. I do not want the student to read in class less often; I want more of his readings to be considered preparations rather than presentations–preparations in which both the practitioner and the critic focus on problems of technique. When I say presentations are too limited in conception, I mean that students should be exposed more frequently—in what they react to and in what they are asked to attempt—to the creative emphasis inherent in confronting their own individual role as communicators. This, too, is related to criticism, for it demands the development of a new set or at least an enlarged set of evaluative criteria and guidance procedures.

It may be asserted that oral interpretation, as a field of study, does not share with the physical, biological, and behavioral sciences the need to cope with an overwhelming expansion of knowledge. In one sense this is true but not in another sense. Moreover, I can easily maintain that even the sense in which it is true is essentially irrelevant in the determination of our attitudes and procedures. Both facets of this warrant more careful consideration.

In what sense is it not true that interpretation is a relatively static field with a compact body of knowledge? The answer lies in the fact that interpretation is an activity which relates literature to the communicative needs of an individual in a social context. Clearly, nobody can seek to teach or to learn all the information that is and will be available about the total body of literature or the communicative needs of the individual within a society. Not only is the body of literature immense and the needs complex but both are constantly changing. On the very simplest level, no student of interpretation can possibly study how to interpret every work of literature; of necessity, he must seek concepts and procedures that are applicable to the literature and the interpretative tasks he has yet to confront.

In what sense is the relatively static dimension of interpretation irrelevant to our attitudes and procedures? It is irrelevant to the degree that we seek to develop people who can interpret materials not previously known to them and to employ interpretation as a communicative resource available and useful throughout their lives. It is irrelevant, in other words, when we refuse to define the development of an interpreter in terms of coaching somebody to interpret effectively a specific number of "pieces" for a limited number of generally artificial situations (including the highly artificial situation of a formal class).

Our need, therefore, is first to determine the essential body of information to be taught and the essential techniques to be mastered. Then we must seek maximum effectiveness in helping students to learn this information and to master these techniques. The nature of both the information and the techniques as well as the degree to which technical mastery should be achieved will depend on whether our primary concern is with artists, audiences, or educated and skillful communicators. Finally, we must infuse the student with a desire to apply his learning and his techniques. In this three-fold drive for knowledge, skill, and motivation, we must strive for greater success in certain areas than we usually achieve. We must gain knowledge of the communication process and of standards of effectiveness. We must practice techniques. We must relate our communicative techniques to our social needs and, as a consequence, to our social and personal value systems. We must develop a critical sense as an integral part of our study, teaching or practice of interpretation.

In conclusion, I would warn the reader to avoid three pitfalls. First, do not confuse the manner in which my remarks relate to the objective techniques of analysis with the manner in which they relate to the less objective procedures of evaluation and prescription. Second, do not perceive alternatives to complete objectivity as necessarily mysterious or unsystematic. Third, do not react to the lack of supporting material presented here in such a way as to lessen your receptivity (under the mistaken notion that I have been trying to convince you). The essential point of this chapter is that the need for a systematic critical method should not make us avoid subjectivity or value judgments but it should impose on the critic the necessity to delineate the basis for his judgments; only in this way is it possible for others to estimate the validity of a critical system and the skill with which, in any given instance, it is applied. In making this point, I have not sought to prove anything but to probe a sufficient number of facets of the problem to accomplish the objectives set forth in the first sentence of the chapter.

FURTHER READINGS

BOOKS

Abrams, M. H., *The Mirror and the Lamp: Romantic Theory and the Critical Tradition.* W. W. Norton and Company, Inc., New York, 1958.
Braden, Waldo W. ed., *Speech Methods and Resources: A Textbook for the Teacher of Speech.* Harper and Row, Publishers, 1961.
Brooks, Keith, Eugene Bahn, and L. LaMont Okey, *The Communicative Act of Oral Interpretation.* Allyn and Bacon, Inc., Boston, 1967.
Cobin, Martin, *Theory and Techniques of Interpretation.* Prentice-Hall, Inc., 1959.
Frye, Northrop, *Anatomy of Criticism.* Princeton University Press, Princeton, New Jersey, 1957.
Grace, William, *Response to Literature.* McGraw-Hill Book Company, Inc., New York, 1965.
Greene, Theodore M., *The Arts and the Art of Criticism.* Princeton University Press, Princeton, New Jersey, 1940.
Stallman, R. W. ed., *Critiques and Essays in Criticism.* The Ronald Press, New York, 1949.
Veilleux, Jere, *Oral Interpretation: The Re-creation of Literature.* Harper and Row Publishers, New York, 1967.

Chapter VIII

THE RESEARCH: A BEHAVIORAL APPROACH

Paul D. Brandes

This final chapter considers the possible contributions of experimental research to oral interpretation and offers two behavioral studies as examples.

A t Emory University, a new field of study, engineering medicine, is developing. For many years physicians have sensed the inadequacy of the machinery needed in surgery and therapy, but they have lacked the mechanical ability to design what was needed. The program at Emory University will provide medicine with personnel holding a degree in medicine and a degree in engineering, providing a union of two skills to produce much needed research.

If experimental method is to make its proper contribution to the oral interpretation of literature, a similar union of programs of studies must take place. Clevenger pointed out that all research in speech is interdisciplinary in that "research in speech often requires information and methods from disciplines that are entirely outside the field of speech."[1] Colleges and universities must develop persons skilled in the art of oral interpretation and skilled in the science of controlled research. It is needless to argue in the twentieth century that these skills are incompatible. We will have doctors trained in engineering, scientists trained in diplomacy, and artists trained in the physics of color. And we will have an increasing number of persons in oral interpretation who can perform experimental research. It is also needless to argue that the education of such specialists will be time-consuming and expensive. There is both the time and the money for scholars to develop dual skills. Our training institutions must see to it that such dual specialists are developed. In 1949 Bacon noted: "Interpretation. . . seems to some students not susceptible of development on the graduate level, because they regard it as an art which depends upon creative talent rather than upon scholarship. . . ."[2] The union of art and science in behavioral studies in oral interpretation is one way to demonstrate that oral interpretation is a suitable field for graduate research.

Once given the researcher trained in both oral interpretation and in experimental method, what areas of study deserve his immediate attention? Four fields of research obviously need further study: pedagogy, technique, therapy, and occupational research. The first report which follows this introductory essay is an experimental study in pedagogy. It explores one facet of the important question, How can the oral interpretation of literature be taught more effectively? In a study of pedagogy considerable attention must be given to all three phases of teaching; the teacher, the subject matter, and the student. Among the problems pertaining to the teacher are the following:

1. How can the high school teacher of English be most expediently trained in oral interpretation? What films can be developed? How much progress can be made in a summer institute?
2. To what extent do courses in voice and diction contribute to effective oral interpretation? Should voice and diction be a prerequisite to oral interpretation?
3. What personal properties and/or academic backgrounds contribute most to an effective teacher of oral interpretation?
4. How can the teacher of oral interpretation and the teacher of English literature most effectively combine their talents in a team-reaching effort?

The academic world is going to demand an increasingly efficient teacher. Those interested in oral interpretation should assist in answering the questions of how the teacher of oral interpretation can be trained more effectively, and how others not specialists in the field, can be provided with the skills to make them effective teachers.

The subject matter to be discussed in the classroom deserves much scrutiny. Here are five hypotheses concerning content which could be tested experimentally:

1. The oral interpretation of Shakespeare improves skills more than does the oral interpretation of contemporary poetry.
2. Students who listen outside of class to recordings of literature to be read in class are students who put less of their own imagination into their readings.
3. Students who interpret long selections learn skills faster than students who interpret short selections.
4. Students who study how to interpret one poet through a semester learn skills faster than students who read from a variety of poets through a semester.
5. Students who practice reading prose selections exclusively do not improve in their ability to read poetry.

Whether or not difficult selections and more familiar selections are more profitable to the oral interpreter was discussed by Armstrong and Brandes.[3] Many other facets of the subject matter which are most effective in teaching oral interpretation skills need to be explored.

The third area involving the pedagogy of oral interpretation lies with the student himself. Klyn said: "We need to *know* what actually happens to students in an oral interpretation course, and how their relationship with literature and specific literary works is affected."[4] For example, not much is known about which students make more effective oral interpreters. Of particular interest here is the element of empathy. Is there a way to determine which students are more empathic than others? If so, are the more empathic students better interpreters? Can empathy in a student be developed? Are students who score high on certain standardized tests more easily taught oral interpretation than those who score low? At what age can the student most effectively begin the study of oral interpretation? All these questions and many others must be answered before the most effective student for oral interpretation can be singled out.

The second field of research concerning oral interpretation involves the investigation of techniques which produce more effective reading. Research in this field may be divided first into the back-ground work on the selection and then its delivery. It may be possible to investigate whether a knowledge of the author and his other works contributes to the effectiveness of oral reading, whether a critical analysis of the selection contributes to over-all performance, and whether a comprehension of imagery and figures of speech improves the reader's ability to present his material. The second study which follows this introductory essay involves research into the content of the introduction, asking what types of introductions are more effective than others. There are many facets involving content which provide interesting material for research.

A number of hypotheses can be developed pertaining to both phases of delivery, some of which follow:

1. Over-articulation in oral interpretation distracts from effective reading.
2. An audience is not nearly so aware of the reader's movement as is the reader's critic trained in oral interpretation.
3. Eye-contact in some types of literature is much more important than in other types of literature.
4. A reader who is seated at a table is just as effective as a reader who is standing at a podium.
5. The overly sibilant "s" in readers may be eliminated with a series of intensive therapy lessons.
6. Readers with "South of England" dialect are more effective than readers with General American dialect.

It must be expected that considerable effort will be needed before the pieces of the puzzle concerning delivery can be put together. Exploratory researchers in this field must be prepared to have critics term their findings isolated and inconclusive. Only when a number of studies have been accumulated can it be said that research on voice and bodily movement in oral interpretation has become meaningful.

A third field of research concerning oral interpretation relates to the art of therapy. There is room for investigation of the reaction of both normal and abnormal subjects to reading literature aloud. English classes studying Shakespeare in high school and college often read the plays in class. The purpose is not therapeutic, but it may well be that a therapeutic function is involved. What reactions do readers have who involve themselves deeply in a given literary selection? Let us suppose that a class in oral interpretation studies in detail C. S. Lewis'*The Great Divorce*. Will its reaction to personal problems differ significantly from students who are not subjected to Lewis' careful scrutiny of heaven and hell? Will such students under Lewis' influence become less self-centered, more benevolent, and more concerned about their salvation? The relationship between role playing and oral interpretation has yet to be established. The oral interpreter is a role player, for he becomes much more involved in the selection than does the silent reader. Psychological experimentation is becoming more and more interested in subjects who must assume a direct responsibility for advocating an issue, even though the point of view they must take is directly opposed to their own personal opinions. Suppose oral interpreters who had racial prejudice were asked to interpret selections aimed to reduce their bias? Would measurable shift-of-opinion take place from their role playing process?

A new but not entirely separate field is available concerning the effect of oral interpretation on abnormal subjects. At one state hospital a reading hour was organized at which patients reported aloud and read aloud from the books that they had been reading. Although no attempt was made to measure the therapeutic effects of such an hour, the hospital authorities were enthusiastic about its continuation. It would require only a minimum amount of effort to measure the effect of such reading hours on the mental attitude of patients. Suppose that tape recordings or records of orally interpreted literature were made available to a variety of patients in mental hospitals? Suppose that college students reporting anxieties were asked to read certain selections aloud to their clinician? Would the therapeutic results be measurable?

The vocational aspects of oral interpretation are inspiring to the researcher. For example, what types of short courses would be more effective in improving the ability of ministers to read aloud from the Bible? To what extent are ministers satisfied with their present Bible reading efforts? How desirous are they of improving their reading habits? What sort of course work would they be more amenable to?[5]

Furthermore, how can the professional man, (the physician, the engineer, the scientist) be made a more effective reader of his scholarly papers? What training in oral reading has he had? What training in oral reading does he think he needs? Under what conditions will he respond more effectively to instruction? Will he respond better if he is taught by one of his own colleagues or will he respond effectively to instruction by an expert in oral interpretation? These are only a few of the aspects of research involving vocational training and oral interpretation.

The possibilities for controlled research in the field of oral interpretation are limitless. There is no inherent incompatibility between carefully planned science and effective art. What is needed is personnel trained in both areas. Once given such personnel, research possibilities in pedagogy, technique, therapy, occupations, and other fields become readily apparent.

The two experimental studies which follow are presented not only for whatever value their content may carry, but as examples of the use of behavioral science research in oral interpretation.

RETENTION OF THE CONTENT OF LITERATURE IN A CLASS IN ORAL INTERPRETATION

Paul D. Brandes

Although the practice of teachers of oral interpretation varies considerably, it can be said that by far the majority of instructors do not hold their students responsible for the content of the selections read during the class. The emphasis in the course is largely upon how to read the selection and not upon what the selection is about. The question often asked is whether a second objective of the course (teaching the content of the selections) is incompatible with teaching how to read the selections. Would the motivational factor of examining students on the content of the selection result in improved retention of the content of the literature, and, if so, what ramifications would this increased knowledge of content have upon student attitudes? Instructors in literature in the field of English generally expect both an improvement in the ability to read literature silently and an improvement in the knowledge of the content of the selections. Can the instructor in oral interpretation expect the same results without weakening his instruction on the technique of reading aloud?

In order to answer the first question, four classes in the oral interpretation of literature of approximately twenty students each, offered during the fall of 1963 at Ohio University, were assigned two prose units.[1] The first unit was presented in the conventional manner. Subjects were assigned a selection from a paperback anthology of short stories purchased by everyone in the class, were told to develop a proficiency in reading the particular selection assigned to them, and were graded on the way in which they read the selection. At the conclusion of the first unit, without warning, a twenty-question test was given to determine the degree to which the students had learned the content of the selections read in class.

106

When the second unit on prose was announced, subjects were warned forcefully that they would be graded not only on the quality of their reading, but also on their ability to retain the content of the literature. Each instructor was left free to present this motivational appeal in his own manner, but it was agreed that stress would be placed upon getting the subjects to study the literature outside of the class period. At the conclusion of the second unit, a twenty-question test was again administered to determine the retention of content. Tests were identical as to the types of questions used, but differed according to the content in keeping with the literature read.

In order to insure that a difference in the difficulty of the units would not affect the results, three experts outlined two units of work, Unit A and Unit B, which the experts felt were of equal difficulty. Assignments were then counter-balanced. Unit A was studied by two groups without the threat appeal at the same time that Unit B was studied by two groups without the threat appeal; then Unit A was assigned to two of the groups which were threatened with the examination, and Unit B to the other two groups which were threatened. (See Figure One) A counter-balancing of the two tests was also achieved by this procedure, so that, if the test on Unit A was more difficult than the test on Unit B, the difference would not affect the results. However, every effort was made to keep the tests of equal difficulty.

EFFECT UPON RETENTION OF CONTENT

Table One shows the analysis of variance for the random replications design as applied to the over-all results of the twenty-question test.[2] The mean number of mistakes out of 20 questions for the group not motivated by an examination was 7.15, while the mean number of mistakes out of 20 questions for the group motivated by an examination was 5.13.[3]

In order to determine what sort of content was being retained, the twenty questions were divided into two groups. Ten questions (five multiple choice and five completion) were categorized as simple recall items, while ten other questions (five multiple choice and five completion) were labeled as thought items. The analysis of variance for the random replications design was applied to each of the two groups. Results for the recall questions were signigicantly different in favor of the motivated groups at the .05 level, while results for the thought questions were similarly significant at the .01 level. Thus, the threat appeal not only increased the recall of content, but it also improved the ability of the students to associate ideas as is indicated by the improved scores on the thought questions. The significant difference on the thought questions is of particular interest to the field of oral interpretation, since total comprehension of literature is one of the goals being sought by teachers of oral interpretation.

Furthermore, a breakdown of the questions into ten completion questions and ten multiple choice questions showed that, when an analysis was run using the ten multiple choice questions only, results between the tested subjects and the non-tested subjects were not significant, whereas significance was achieved in comparing the two groups on the ten completion questions only. Thus, the motivational factor of being required to learn the content of the literature was able to elicit a greater response when subjects were free to think about the questions, whereas there was no difference when multiple choice answers were involved. The suggestable quality of the multiple choice questions may have been sufficient to remind subjects of content which was on the fringes of their memory.

EFFECT UPON ATTITUDES

Assuming that the threat has been successful in increasing the degree to which subjects learned the content of the selections, what side effects resulted? When subjects were asked how much they had enjoyed listening to the selections, there was no significant difference between their enjoyment of the unit with the retention test at the end and their enjoyment of the unit without the test. Evidently, the threat of an examination did not detract from the pleasure of the unit, nor did it increase it. Subjects may have delayed improving their knowledge of the selections until just before the examination and therefore were not able to contribute their increased knowledge to an enjoyment of the literature.

When subjects were asked how much pressure they were under in studying for the unit, no significant differences in pressure between the two types of units were reported. Thus, the motivational factor of an examination was successful in eliciting improved learning of content without making the subjects feel a difference in pressure of study.

Subjects also stated that they did not spend significantly more time on the unit with the retention test than they did on the unit without the retention test, nor did they feel that they had made more improvement in their oral reading during one unit than they had during the other.

	No Threat	Threat
Class 1	A	B
Class 2	B	A
Class 3	A	B
Class 4	B	A

FIGURE ONE

Counter-Balancing of Units A and B

TABLE ONE

Summary Table of Analysis of Variance for Total Retention

Source	df	ss	ms	F
Treatments	1	8.22	8.22	24.90*
Replications	3	24.43	8.14	
Interaction	3	.98	.33	
Total	7	33.63		

*significant at the .05 level of significance

Thus, the motivational factor of a rentention test did secure increased learning without adding side effects which might be injurious to the appreciation of reading literature aloud.

SUMMARY

This study asked whether the motivational factor of an examination would increase retention of the content of selections read in classes in the oral interpretation of literature and what side-effects might result from the test. Significant differences were reported in retention in favor of the motivated groups. The difference was significant when questions were broken down into ten recall items and ten thought items, but, when the questions were divided according to completion and multiple-choice items, significance was achieved only for the ten completion items.

No differentiating side—effects were reported. Subjects enjoyed the selections in one group as much as they did in the other. Subjects felt under no more pressure in one group than they did in the other, nor did they differentiate in the time they said they had spent on the units or in the improvement in oral reading that they thought they had made.

Therefore, students in classes in oral interpretation can have their knowledge of the literature increased by being threatened by a retention test without contributing side-effects which detract from effective instruction in the techniques of reading aloud. Further study is needed to see if these results are limited to the type of subject and the type of literature involved in this experiment. A more objective evaluation of success in reading aloud other than the subjects' own opinions of their improvement may well show that the improved learning of content also results in an improved oral performance.

FOOTNOTES
(Study Number One)

[1] All selections were taken from the paperback, *Seventy-Five Short Masterpieces: Stories from the World's Literature*, ed. R. B. Goodman (New York: Bantam Books, 1961). In order to observe time limits and to maintain equality of difficulty, subjects were assigned the exact number of lines to read. At times, more than one subject was assigned to a given short story in order to provide continuity for the narrative.

[2] In order to conserve space, summary tables for the data as broken down into thought and recall questions and into completion and multiple-choice questions have been omitted.

[3] Two experts graded all questions. Agreement on which answers were correct was achieved without major difficulty.

THE EFFECT OF THE INTRODUCTION ON A LITERARY COMMUNICATION

Paul D. Brandes, University of North Carolina

Marie Shepardson, United States Office of Information, Pakistan

The studies of Cromwell,[1] Sponberg,[2] and Luchins[3] on the laws of primacy and recency have shown that introductory material influences a subsequent communication. Janis, Lumsdaine and Gladstone[4] reported that prefatory material may reduce the fear reaction to a subsequent threat appeal; while Hovland and Mandell,[5] Ewing,[6] and Kelman and Hovland[7] have demonstrated that an introduction may modify communicator creadibility. Many other interactions of prefatory material with an ensuing communication remain to be investigated. The purpose of this study is to explore one such interaction, namely, will the type of introduction to a complicated communication of established literary merit affect the retention of the communication? It was hypothesized that an introduction which presents sufficient content, without detracting from the element of suspense, would result in more retention than would an introduction which is artistically sound but which forces the listener to orient himself to the complicated communication without assistance.

Four hypotheses were established: first, the retention of factual material, in a complicated communication of established literary merit, would be greater following a narrative introduction than following an artistic introduction; second, the ability to answer thought questions, based on a complicated communication of established literary merit, would be greater following a narrative introduction than following an artistic introduction; third, the total response to a complicated communication of established literary merit, including both retention of factual material and the ability to answer thought questions, would be greater following a narrative introduction than following an artistic introduction; and fourth, the

*Portions reprinted from*The Quarterly Journal of Speech,* April, 1967, by permission of Speech Association of America.

attitude shift toward the selection, its author, and the reader would be more favorable following a narrative introduction than following an artistic introduction.

PROCEDURE

Robert Browning's monologue, "My Last Duchess," was chosen as the communication because of its complexity, its brevity, its literary merit, and its suitability to both simple retention-question testing and thought-question testing. Two introductions of approximately four hundred words were prepared. The first, known hereafter as the "artistic" introduction, obeyed the laws of units, coherence, and emphasis and was aimed to give subjects the conventional receptive "set" for listening. The historical background of the poem was discussed, as well as the literary type in which Browning wrote his monologues. Little or no discussion of the action of the poem was included. In short, it was the type of introduction commonly given to literary selections. The second introduction, termed here the "narrative" introduction, was designed to accomplish the objectives of unity, coherence, and emphasis, but also to acquaint subjects with the circumstances of the story to a degree which would enhance their understanding of the poem without removing the factor of suspense. The several characters in the poem were introduced and their personalities were discussed. The phraseology of the poem was used whenever possible so that the listeners would become acquainted with the vocabulary which they were to hear. Care was taken, however, not to reveal the answers to any of the questions to be included in the criterion measure.

Seven readers, ranging in skill from moderate to high, were trained to deliver the introductions and the poem. Intensive rehearsals assured a relatively skillful performance and made certain that the independent variable was successfully executed. The experimenters were satisfied that all the readers were proficient before the experiment began.

A post-test of eighteen questions was administered after each of the fourteen readings. The ten open-ended questions listed below were a random distribution of five simple retention questions and five thought questions:

1. What question did visitors ask the Duke about the Duchess's picture?
2. In your opinion, what does the Duke believe his speaking ability to be?

3. In addition to considering Fra Pandolf a great artist, what was the Duke's opinion of Fra Pandolf?

4. What was the Duke's attitude toward the way in which the Duchess thanked people for favors they did her?

5. What evidence is there in the poem that the Duke is more interested in the financial arrangements of the marriage than in the future bride?

6. In the Duke's opinion, what should have made the Duchess smile?

7. How does the Duke describe the Duchess's heart?

8. How old was the Duke's name?

9. What was the Duke's attitude toward telling the Duchess about the things which annoyed him?

10. What does the Duke say with regard to his speaking ability?

The last eight of the eighteen questions attempted to measure the audience attitude toward the reader, the selection, and the author. For example question eleven read; What is your opinion of this poem? Subjects were permitted to choose from among five answers, ranging from *outstanding to poor.*

The 240 subjects used for the study were members of four speech courses in progress at Ohio University during the spring semester of 1961: beginning oral communication, public speaking, history of the visual theatre, and history of oratory. Readers were assigned at random to one of seven replications, each replication requiring the reader to deliver the communication with the artistic introduction to one group and with the narrative introduction to a second group. Populations were held constant within any one replication. Treatment sequence within a replication was randomized.

Three experts graded the ten open-ended questions independently. A conference was held in which scores were compared. All inconsistencies, most of which were minor, were resolved. However, in the course of the discussions, it was decided that question five, a thought question, would have to be struck, because a portion of the narrative introduction was being used by subjects to offer a suitable answer to the question. The analysis of the data, therefore, was limited to four thought questions and five retention questions.

ANALYSIS OF RESULTS

Data was analyzed using the analysis of variance for the random replications design. Using mean scores, all hypotheses were retained.

The nonsignificance of the interaction, F=msAR/msw, permitted the development of a pooled error term and the testing of F based upon raw scores[8] for the data based upon the five retention questions and for the combined thought and retention scores. Computations were performed on the IBM 360 computer to five decimal places.

Table One shows the results of comparing the scores on the five factual questions only. The mean score of the 120 subjects who heard the communication prefaced by the artistic introduction was 1.83; while the mean score of the 120 subjects who heard the communication prefaced by the narrative introduction was 1.99. Using a pooled error term, the difference, although in the predicted direction, did not reach significance at the .05 level.

Table Two shows the results of comparing scores on the four thought questions only. The mean score for the artistic introduction 1.61; while the mean score for the narrative introduction was 1.99. The F obtained by using the random replications, mean scores design did not reach significance at the .05 level, although the difference in means was again in the predicted direction. A significant interaction precluded using a pooler error term to test for main effects.

Table Three shows the results by combining the scores on the five retention questions and the four thought questions. Using a pooled error term to compute main effects, the difference in favor of the narrative introduction was significant at the .05 level of confidence. The data, therefore, supported the third hypothesis.

An analysis of the combined scores on the eight attitude questions failed to show any differences between introductions.

INTERPRETATION OF RESULTS

Under the conditions established for the study, an introduction which makes a specific effort to acquaint the audience with detail was found to be more effective in improving retention of a complicated literary communication of established merit than was an introduction which, although artistically sound, was lacking in specifics. This difference was not apparent when responses to factual questions and responses to thought questions were analyzed separately, but was manifested when scores on factual and thought questions were pooled. Attitudes toward the reader, the author, and the selection showed no significant differences between the two treatments, perhaps because of the brevity of the communications.

APPLICATION OF THE RESULTS

Prefatory material to a complex communication can significantly affect the comprehension of the communication. Ideas not presented in the introduction can be illuminated by auxilary material which is included in the introduction. Further research should attempt to determine under what conditions these findings will hold true. Of particular interest is the degree to which improved comprehension of a communication affects attitudes toward that communication. The negative findings of this study may not hold true under a situation which permits more time for subjects to adjust their attitudes.

TABLE ONE

Summary Table for Retention of Fact

Source	df	ss	ms	F
Treatments	1	2.40	2.40	1.33
Replications	6	18.63		
Cells		27.66		
Interactions	6	6.63	1.10	.61
Within	226	4111.52	1.82	
Total		439.18		

Since the $ms_{interaction}$ and the ms_{within} were approximately the same, it is possible to assume no interaction. Therefore, the F was tested by obtaining a ms_{pooled} error term by adding the $ss_{interaction}$ and the ss_{within} and dividing by the combined degrees of freedom.

TABLE TWO

Summary Table for Thought Questions

Source	df	SS	ms	F
Treatments	1	11.27	11.27	
Replications	6	11.94		
Cells		47.84		
Interactions	6	24.63	4.11	2.77*
Within	226	334.76	1.48	
Total		382.60		

*significant at the .05 level. This significant interaction precludes use of raw scores to test the difference between treatments.

TABLE THREE

Summary Table for Fact and Thought Questions

Source	df	SS	ms	F
Treatments	1	22.20	22.20	4.37*
Replications	6	39.14		
Cells		103.48		
Interactions	6	42.13	7.02	1.34
Within	226	11137.02	5.02	
Total		1240.50		

*significant at the .05 level using a pooled error term

SUMMARY

Narrative introductory material to a complex communication of established literary merit proved significantly more effective than artistic introductory material, when the criteria for measurement consisted of nine short-answer completion questions, five of which called for simple retention and four for associated responses. The difference was not sustained when scores on the retention questions and on the thought questions were analyzed separately. No significant difference was found in the attitudes of subjects toward the reader, the author, and the selection, when those attitudes were measured by a composite score based on eight attitude responses.

FOOTNOTES
(Study Number Two)

[1]Harvey Cromwell, "The Relative Effect of Audience Attitude of the First Versus the Second Argumentative Speech of a Series," *Speech Monographs,* XVII (June, 1950), pp. 105-122, and Harvey Cromwell, "The Persistency of the Effect on Audience Attitude of the First Versus the Second Argumentative Speech of a Series," *Speech Monographs,* XXI (November, 1954), pp. 280-284.

[2]Harold Sponberg, "A Study of the Relative Effectiveness of Climax and Anti-Climax Order in an Argumentative Speech," *Speech Monographs,* XIII (No. 1, 1946), pp. 35-44.

[3]A. S. Luchins, "Definiteness of Impression and Primacy-Recency Communications," *Order of Presentation,* ed. C. I. Hovland (New Haven, 1957), pp. 33-61, A. S. Luchins, "Experimental Attempts to Minimize the Impact of First Impressions," *Order of Presentation,* ed. C. I.Hovland (New Haven, 1957), pp. 62-75.

[4]I. L. Janis, A. A. Lumadaine, and A. I. Gladstone, "Effects of Preparatory Communications on Reactions to a Subsequent News Event," *Public Opinion Quarterly,* XV (Fall, 1951), pp. 487-518.

[5]C. I. Hovland and W. Mandell, "An Experimental Comparison of Conclusion-Drawing by the Communicator and by the Audience," *Journal of Abnormal and Social Psychology,* XLVII (July, 1951), pp. 581-588.

[6]T. N. Ewing, "A Study of Certain Factors Involved in Changes of Opinion," *Journal of Social Psychology,* XVI (February, 1942), pp. 63-88.

[7]H. C. Kelman and C. I. Hovland, "Reinstatement of the Communicator in Delayed Measurement of Opinion Changes," *Journal of Abnormal and Social Psychology,* XLVIII (July, 1953), pp. 327-335.

[8]E. F. Lindquist, *The Design and Analysis of Experiments in Psychology and EEducation,* (Boston, 1956), pp. 190-202. Subjects in the two large fine arts classes were divided randomly into eight groups. The smaller classes were used as intact units.

CHAPTER FOOTNOTES

[1]Theodore Clevenger, Jr., "Research Opportunities in Speech," *Introduction to the Field of Speech,* ed. R. F. Reid (Chicago, 1965), p. 213.

[2]Wallace A. Bacon, "Graduate Studies in Interpretation", *Quarterly Journal of Speech,* XXXV (October, 1949), p. 316.

[3]Chloe Armstrong and Paul D. Brandes, *The Oral Interpretation of Literature* (New York, 1963), pp. 36-37.

[4]Mark S. Klyn, "Potentials for Research in Oral Interpretation," *Western Speech,* XXIX (Winter, 1965), p. 103.

[5]Bacon, *op. cit.* p. 318.

FURTHER READINGS

BOOKS

Berlo, David K., *The Process of Communication.* Holt, Rinehart and Winston, Inc., New York, 1960.

Cofer, Charles N., *Verbal Learning and Verbal Behavior.* McGraw-Hill Book Company, Inc., New York, 1961.

Underwood, Benton, J. and Rudolph W. Schultz, *Meaning and Verbal Learning.* J. B. Lippincott Company, Philadelphia, 1956.

Wiener, Norbert, *The Human Use of Human Beings.* Doubleday and Company, Inc., New York, 1956.

Yule, G. Udny, *The Statistical Study of Literary Vocabulary.* The University Press, Cambridge, England, 1944.

ARTICLES

Grigsby, O. J., An Experimental Study of the Development of Concepts of Relationship in Pre-school Children as Evidenced by their Expressive Ability," *Journal of Experimental Education,* Vol. 1, Swcember, 1932, pp. 144-162.

Skinner, B. F., "The Alliteration in Shakespeare's Sonnets: A Study in Literary Behavior," *Psychological Record,* Vol. 3, pp. 186-192.